D1606398

ALDEN NOWLAN

Selected Poems

ALSO BY ALDEN NOWLAN

POETRY
A Darkness in the Earth
The Rose and the Puritan
Under the Ice
Wind in a Rocky Country
The Things Which Are
Bread, Wine and Salt
The Mysterious Naked Man
Playing the Jesus Game
Between Tears and Laughter
I'm a Stranger Here Myself
Smoked Glass
I Might Not Tell Everybody This
The Gardens of the Wind
Alden Nowlan: Early Poems

FICTION
Miracle at Indian River
Various Persons Called Kevin O'Brien
Nine Micmac Legends
Will Ye Let the Mummers In?
The Wanton Troopers

NONFICTION
Shaped by This Land (with Tom Forrestall)
Campobello
Double Exposure

DRAMA
Frankenstein (with Walter Learning)
The Incredible Murder of Cardinal Tosca
(with Walter Learning)

ALDEN NOWLAN

Selected Poems

EDITED AND WITH AN INTRODUCTION BY
PATRICK LANE AND LORNA CROZIER

First published in 1996 by
House of Anansi Press Limited
34 Lesmill Road
Toronto, ON M3B 2T6
Tel. (416) 445-3333
Fax (416) 445-5967
www.anansi.ca

Distributed in Canada by
General Distribution Services Inc.
325 Humber College Blvd.
Etobicoke, ON, M9W 7C3
Tel. (416) 213-1919
Fax (416) 213-1917
E-mail cservice@genpub.com

04 03 02 01 00   2 3 4 5 6

Canadian Cataloguing in Publication Data

Nowlan, Alden, 1933–1983
Alden Nowlan selected poems
ISBN 0-88784-573-8
I.. Lane, Patrick, 1939–   . II. Crozier, Lorna, 1948–   . III Title.
PS8527.09A6 1995 C811'.54 C95-931800-3
PR9199.3.N68A6   1995

Cover design: the boy 100 and Tannice Goddard

THE CANADA COUNCIL | LE CONSEIL DES ARTS
FOR THE ARTS | DU CANADA
SINCE 1957 | DEPUIS 1957

*We acknowledge for their financial support of our
publishing program the Canada Council for the Arts,
the Ontario Arts Council, and the Government of Canada through
the Book Publishing Industry Development Program (BPIDP).*

Printed and bound in Canada

Contents

Foreword

ALDEN NOWLAN WAS BORN IN 1933 in Stanley, Nova Scotia. His young mother, who was fifteen when Alden was born, gave him to his father and grandmother to raise. He went to school for only five years, leaving when he was twelve years old to work as a pulp cutter and millhand in the forests of the Maritimes. Nowlan was a child of the Depression, a time of poverty and struggle. It had a powerful effect upon him and upon his writing. During the early years he read voluminously, consuming the books in the library of Windsor, Nova Scotia. Like many writers of his generation, including Al Purdy and Milton Acorn, Nowlan was largely self-educated and read across the spectrum of literature and history.

At nineteen, Nowlan left the bush and got a job with a small-town paper in Hartland, New Brunswick. For the next eleven years he worked as a journalist while also writing poems and publishing them in literary journals across Canada and the United States. By the time he left Hartland in 1963 to work in Saint John for the *Telegraph-Journal* he had published five books and was generally recognized as a fine poet, one of the best of his generation. Three years later he had surgery for throat cancer, and the following year his book *Bread, Wine and Salt* won the Governor General's Award for poetry.

I first met Alden in 1967 or '68. We met at a party at his home on the hill by the University of New Brunswick. I fell quite in love with Claudine, his wife, and danced and drank, entranced by the spirit of his home and his other guests. Al Pittman and Ray Fraser were there and so was Louis Cormier. I was a young poet hardly anyone had ever heard of and he was kind to me. Towards midnight he made me an honourary Maritimer, everyone in the room solemnly raising their glasses to his bidding.

At three in the morning he stripped me of the honour, calling me a West Coast intellectual and a fool. Everyone solemnly drank to that as well. By five in the morning we were all singing songs, maudlin and in our cups. I've never had an honour so bestowed and so quickly stripped away.

We met many times over the following years. I saw him last in the spring of 1983, two months before he died. He was very sick. I knew that he knew me, but he was at that point far along in the illness that would lead him to his death. I loved the man and loved his poetry. It is fair to say that he was one of the beloved of this earth. I knew him as such and I treasure his memory, the moments we had together talking of poetry and life. Whether I was sitting in a chair in his living room sharing a glass of gin or a beer with him and Claudine, or sitting with him four thousand miles away, his poems spoke softly to me, moving me to a place as close to the heart as anyone has. I thank him for that.

PATRICK LANE

Introduction

Alden Nowlan 1933–1983

IN THE MIDDLE OF THE EIGHTH CENTURY, Tu Fu wrote a poem that
he dedicated to a friend and fellow writer. It voices the com-
plaints we still hear from poets twelve hundred years later —
lack of money, lack of recognition — yet the final lines offer
some comfort:

> Our poems will be handed
> Down along with great dead poets'.
> We can console each other.
> At least we shall have descendants.

We think these ancient lines seem a worthy tribute to Alden
Nowlan, for his descendants already include two generations.
So often we have heard students say that in their studies of the
classic Canadian anthologies it is Alden's work that stands out,
his poems they remember and take into their lives as messages
of love and wisdom. His poetry lives on in the words of many
of us who write today; his voice will grace our lives for years
to come.

Alden's poems continue to be published, read and talked
about not only because he was a skilled craftsman and immacu-
late writer, but also because he had a great heart. Our literature
has not produced another like him, none with the gift of such
honesty and insight, and such a wry recognition of human
frailties. The character that speaks in his best poems is some-
times awkward, contradictory or ashamed, but he is always
genuine, and he expresses a compassion that is deeply felt.
Although it is suspect to equate this speaker with the poet

himself, a reader can't help but feel that it is Alden Nowlan talking. The voice in the poem, with all its flaws, uncertainties and desires, is his. In the poems of Robert Frost, to whom Nowlan has frequently been compared, we sense the poet speaking behind a mask, as if he has fabricated his avuncular, bucolic narrator who lectures us with the moral authority of his Puritan past. While Nowlan shares Frost's plain speech and his fascination with rural prejudices and values, he chose a different tact; he comes out of that same Northeastern Puritanism, but his voice rings with humility, self-doubt and tenderness, a tone that never betrays the heart. In later poems, such as "Great Things Have Happened," he speaks so clearly and directly that he might be sitting at your kitchen table, glass in hand, simply talking. How privileged a reader feels to be in the presence of such intimate, eloquent stories.

This lack of distance between the man and his words was not always the case. Nowlan's early poems, shaped as they are by strict rhyme and metre, are more restrained and formal, but their subject matter rises directly out of the world in which he grew up; small-town rural Nova Scotia and New Brunswick. Though Nowlan writes of the people and places where he lived, in these early pieces he is far from the common speech he utilizes later. In "Warren Pryor," a poem reminiscent of E. A. Robinson's "Richard Corey," Nowlan writes of a young man whose parents have laboured to free him from the hard work and poverty of the farm, "the meagre acreage that bore them down." Warren Pryor graduates from school to work in the bank, "saved / from their thistle-strewn farm and its red dirt." Nowlan skillfully uses concurrent stresses and masculine end rhymes to create the angry tension that culminates in the last stanza:

> And he said nothing. Hard and serious
> like a young bear inside his teller's cage,
> his axe-hewn hands upon the paper bills
> aching with empty strength and throttled rage.

Nowlan's more distanced stance in the poems that make up his first four books cannot be equated with objectivity. Without a doubt, this writer cares about his subjects and does not withdraw himself from the emotional impact of their experiences; yet his choice of form and point of view keep him slightly removed.

It was in the late 1950s that Nowlan's style began to change. His friend and fellow poet Robert Gibbs explains this shift in his introduction to the 1985 edition of Nowlan's selected poems. Gibbs writes: "In his mature verse Nowlan reaches toward pure poetry, what might be called unmediated speech. Its simplicity is that of truth, the poet's own truth, as purely stated as it can be" (xvii). With this change in voice came a more open form, the lines freed from the constraints of more formal verse. These innovations in speech and style couldn't help but affect his subject matter. As Gibbs states, "The freedom he acquired . . . to move between language at its most heightened and distanced to language at its most simple was essential to the growth of the matter of his poetry. Changes in style were changes in perception, in understanding . . . " (xv).

By the publication of his fifth book, *The Things Which Are,* Nowlan had become more intimate with his subjects and more forgiving of himself and others. In the poem "The Grove Beyond the Barley," he writes of coming upon a naked girl sleeping. The hapless voyeur is a character he is fond of. Here, and in many poems that follow, he is a man come upon a gentle intimacy that both startles and delights. He watches the girl for a moment, and before turning away from her he says:

> . . . I hope you do not waken,
> before I go; one who chooses
> so dark a place
> to lie naked
> might cry out. The shadows quicken,
> I wish you a lover,

> dreams of sunlit meadows,
> imagine myself a gentle satyr.

In transitional poems like this, Alden seems to be delighting in his exploration of the line as a unit of meaning and rhythm freed from the restrictions of accentual-syllabic verse. He begins to play upon a dramatic order. Each line moves with the phrasing of speech, forming a kind of music that bears down upon the way we talk intimately to one another. The lines become more concentrated and distilled, forcing us to pay attention, as if someone were speaking in a voice as close to the soul as it can get. Nowlan makes us want to listen closely. Like William Carlos Williams, whom he read with care and admiration, he is not outside his subject, but inside what he observes — the most dangerous and vulnerable place to be.

Robert Bly, in his introduction to Nowlan's first selected poems, *Playing the Jesus Game*, speaks of Nowlan's courage, a quality we don't often talk about when we discuss poetry. Bly berates the false optimism of much American verse. The alternative, he writes, is "to allow the fear or fears to come forward into the poem unconquered." Bly claims that Nowlan does this in Canadian poetry, remarking, "I think his work is the work of a brave man." Bly further explains Nowlan's appeal: ". . . his details are fantastically clear. His clear direct language is not transformative — it's not about one thing changing into another — but a descriptive language, about the way things are." This description is true of most of Nowlan's poetry, and if the poet had done nothing else but show us the way things are that surely would have been enough.

There are many poems, however, that we would call transformative; among them are "Party at Bannon Brook," "The First Stirring of the Beasts" and "I, Icarus." All three take us deep into the mystery of change. In the first, Nowlan speaks of moments when we try to reach past our own isolation to a sense of unity we feel but cannot utter; in the last, he writes of shape shifting and longing; and in "The First Stirring of the Beasts," he touches upon the numinous animal world that we, isolated in our own skin, cannot understand. The transformation poems are among his finest work, for they lead us beyond the edge of our knowing to a place where we touch the gods, a dark world that resides just beyond our hands. "Party at Bannon Brook" brings forth the fear Bly speaks of and leaves us with a haunting sense of primeval power and human dread:

> but because I am afraid. If we could do what we wish,
> always, I would tell them I understand:
> this is the season
> when the bobcat is not driven away
> by smoke, and the eagle
> makes reconnaissance from the coast.

The vast majority of Nowlan's poems explore the everyday, the lives of people whom he often identifies by name. There is Janice Smith, whose husband beats her because her beauty and sensuality enrage the Puritan sensibilities of their town; there is Mary Talbot, who brings flowers to her own grave, ready and waiting beside her husband in the Hainesville Cemetery. There are Aunt Jane, Georgie and Fenwick Cranston, the elusive Nancy and eight generations of Hungerfords, McGards and Staceys. Nowlan's ability to individualize, to put flesh and bone in the lines of his poetry, is raised to the level of genius in "Ypres: 1915." In an amazing tour de force, he ranges through the history of that place: the Moors fleeing, the French "weeping / at the dishonour of it all," the Canadians marching straight for the lines and their imminent deaths in the carnage of shells and gas. The terror of that time and the courage of the Canadians are brilliantly and quietly brought home when the poet moves away from the larger ideas he has developed and centres everything upon one soldier:

Private MacNally thinking:
You squareheaded sons of bitches,
you want this God damn trench
you're going to have to take it away
from Billy MacNally
of the South End of Saint John, New Brunswick.

When Nowlan read the poem out loud, these lines were rich with the accent of the Maritimes, that long drawing-out of the vowels, that sureness of speech, that simplicity of statement. Nowlan's poems about people look deeply and lovingly at those who deserve such a look, but his gaze can also be critical, almost judgemental. Woe to those who speak from a lofty place, whether from the privilege of class or a higher education, as in "The Social Worker's Poem" and "A Mug's Game." He is most critical of those who would deny the beauties of the flesh, the contradictions of being human and the sanctity of the innocent — outcasts like the Jelly Bean Man, who gives children candy "from no other motive than love." Unlike the morally superior people he debunks, he admits his own awkward stumbling towards grace, writing openly of his innermost fears. Poems like "Bobby Sands" show us that he is a man who knows how thin the line is between good and evil.

Many of Nowlan's most moving early poems reveal the sense of shame that dogged his young life, shame arising from his out-of-wedlock birth and his mother's abandonment. In the poem "Beginning" he writes of his conception: "From that they found most lovely, most abhorred, / my parents made me." The poem ends with "never in making was there brighter bliss, / followed by darker shame. Thus I was made." That sense of shame, which revolves around women in much of his work, has more than a personal source. It is one of the characteristics of a generation that grew up in the strict moral order of the puritan Maritimes. Robert Bly talks about fear in Nowlan's poetry: the fear of weakness, of women and the "fear of being exiled, ostracized, [and] put out." It's easy to find all of this in the early books, but in Nowlan's later work much of the anger, bitterness and self-doubt have fallen away, and we are left with what Robert Gibbs has described as "affirmation." This affirmation reveals a quiet and unassuming love of his own country. After the challenge issued by Billy MacNally, "Ypres: 1915" ends with these modest, yet patriotic lines:

> And that's ridiculous, too, and nothing
> on which to found a country.
> > Still
> It makes me feel good, knowing
> that in some obscure, conclusive way
> they were connected with me
> and me with them.

It takes a fine poet to realize that such huge concepts as patriotism and love of country can be eloquently expressed by focusing everything upon a single thing, an image, an ordinary man. Earlier in this poem Nowlan says, "Sometimes I'm not even sure that I have a country." In many brilliant poems such as this, Nowlan writes his country into existence, exploring what it is to be Canadian. One of his shorter pieces, "Canadian January Night," catches that sense of ourselves, our long winters that seem to define who we are.

> Ice storm: the hill
> a pyramid of black crystal
> down which the cars
> slide like phosphorescent beetles
> while I, walking backwards in obedience
> to the wind, am possessed
> of the fearful knowledge
> my compatriots share
> but almost never utter:

>   this is a country
>   where a man can die
>   simply from being
>   caught outside.

Nowlan captures in just a few lines our huge, cold country and the winters we and only a few other countries endure. The poem says something, too, of our distance from one another, the bridge we dare not cross, the reticence, the formality of our loneliness. As much as anything else, Nowlan understood loneliness and loss.

Despite these poems that so explicitly describe Canada and Canadians, for many years Nowlan was known as a "regionalist writer," someone who, because he wrote so intimately about the people and place where he lived, was not considered a writer of the first rank. This perception has done a great disservice both to Nowlan and to Canadian poetry. Almost without exception, great writers draw their material from their own lived experiences. At their most intimate, poets come to their words with an intensity that arises from their bones, the regions of the heart. Nowlan's world is indeed made up of the local, but his neighbourhoods and streets are all settings for exploring a larger humanity. This is what makes Nowlan great. He has the power to reveal our frailties and our loves, the smallness of our behaviour and the largeness of our spirit.

In one of Nowlan's last poems, "He Sits Down on the Floor of a School for the Retarded," he tells the story of going to a school for the mentally handicapped and relates his feelings of awkwardness and helplessness at not knowing quite how to behave. A female resident sits down beside him, puts her arms around him and asks Nowlan to hold her. He is distressed and awkward, unsure of what he should do, and then he does the only human thing he can, he holds her in his arms. He says:

It's what we all want, in the end,
to be held, merely to be held,
to be kissed (not necessarily with the lips,
for every touching is a kind of kiss).

Yes, it's what we all want, in the end,
not to be worshipped, not to be admired,
not to be famous, not to be feared,
not even to be loved, but simply to be held.

It is the rare poet who can reach this far into his understanding of compassion and human need and speak of it so clearly. We are simple creatures, Nowlan tells us, and out of that simplicity we make our lives. At the end of the poem he says of himself, the mentally handicapped woman and anyone who reads his poems: "We are lovers. We are two human beings / huddled together for a little while by the fire / in the Ice Age, two hundred thousand years ago."

PATRICK LANE & LORNA CROZIER

ALDEN NOWLAN

Selected Poems

Hens

Beside the horse troughs, General Grant
swaggered and foraged in the dry manure,
that winter we had twenty-seven hens
graced with white feathers and names of heroes.

Cock of the walk, he took the choicest fodder,
and he was totem, stud and constable
until his comb and spurs were frozen, bled,
and then the hens, quite calmly, picked him dead.

All Down the Morning

All down the morning, women sprinkled crumbs
Of musty laughter, watching Janice Smith
In brazen languor smear her husband's lips
With public kisses, while he glared or blushed.

And when the Sunday village itched in church,
They thought of Janice, hot as Babylon,
Who lured her Jimmie to the porch and bared
His people's blanket-buried secrecies.

Or dancing to the snarl of feline strings,
Each Friday at the school, they leered at jokes
That made obscenities of her taut breasts
Against her startled husband's sweating suit.

For she was city-bred and unaware
That love was bordered by the rumpled quilts
And children bred from duty as the soil
Was ploughed to hide the seed and not for joy.

So taunted by harsh laughter, half-ashamed,
Enraged with rum and manhood late one night,
And shouting like betrayal, Jim came home
To bruise his knuckles on her shameless face.

Weakness

Old mare whose eyes
are like cracked marbles,
drools blood in her mash,
shivers in her jute blanket.

My father hates weakness worse than hail;
in the morning
        without haste
he will shoot her in the ear, once,
shovel her under in the north pasture.

Tonight
        leaving the stables,
he stands his lantern on an over-turned water pail,
turns,
        cursing her for a bad bargain,
and spreads his coat
carefully over her sick shoulders.

In the Hainesville Cemetery

Not all these stones
belong to death. Here and there
you read something
like
>   John Andrew Talbot, 1885–1955
>   Mary, his wife, 1887–

and on decoration day
Mary will come here
and put a jam jar of water and tulips
on her own grave.

> The Talbots are people
> who make the beds before breakfast
> and set the breakfast table
> every night before they go to bed.

After the First Frost

After the first frost.

resting in the cool shadows,
the undisciplined lilac bushes
a green web around her,

old woman in brown stockings,
smelling of wintergreen
a clean burn in my nostrils,
sipping hot milk and ginger,
among the dead lilacs.

Her daughter I knew as a legion of whispers:
how she lay three summers in the hen house,
rocking her simple baby.

And the old woman swept out the hen house with
    spruce boughs,
and built her a hammock from a crazy quilt,
till the baby's head grew
unnatural and huge, and he died.

And the old woman pried him loose from her arms
and laid him on a board between two chairs,
and clothed him in velvet trousers
and a shirt bleached out of flour bags,

and went out to wait in the shadows,
the tilting branches closing around her.

I Knew the Seasons Ere I Knew the Hours

I knew the seasons ere I knew the hours;
the Christmas cactus blossomed anytime
after December first and scarlet flowers
fell patiently, in patterns like the blood
from shallow wounds, in mother's russet parlour.

I was once six and so damned lonely
I called love Rover, he had two sad ears,
a black-white checkerboard of face, a nose
for venison, he stole my uncle blind,
was caught and shot and buried in the pasture.

For months I sprinkled daisies over him,
sucking my grief like lemons. Stephanie
shredded the daisies when she punished me
for being born her brother and we wrestled,
crushing the grass like lovers, till our mother
whipt us apart. Eventually the flowers
were laid less for my grief than for that struggle.

Pussywillows in March

Pussywillows beside the full ditches
blossoming in the season
when the last snow
is more soot than crystal,

there are such curious conflicts
in you, joy and sadness,
and a strange loveliness
in your mud-coloured stalks
and the little blossoms
in their leathery pouches
that are exactly
the colour of an old white shirt
that doesn't look clean
no matter how often you wash it.

God Sour the Milk of the Knacking Wench

God sour the milk of the knacking wench
with razor and twine she comes
to sanchion our blond and bucking bull,
pluck out his lovely plumbs.

God shiver the prunes on her bark of chest,
who capons the prancing young.
Let maggots befoul her alive in bed,
and dibble thorns in her tongue.

For Nicholas of All the Russias

Wind in a rocky country and the harvest
meagre, the sparrows eaten, all the cattle
gone with the ragged troopers, winter coming,
mother will starve for love of you and wrapping
newest and least accustomed leave him squalling
out in the hills beside the skulls of foxes,
it cold and snow in the air. Stranger, knocking,
(now in this latter time even the poor
have bread and sleep on straw) what silly rumour
tells me your eyes are yellow and your lips
once rose trout-quick to suck a she-wolf's teats?

Our Lord, his peaked heir and hawk-faced daughters
are gone, although they say one severed finger
was found after the soldiers cleaned the cellar.

Beginning

From that they found most lovely, most abhorred,
my parents made me: I was born like sound
stroked from the fiddle to become the ward
of tunes played on the bear-trap and the hound.

Not one, but seven entrances they gave
each to the other, and he laid her down
the way the sun comes out. Oh, they were brave,
and then like looters in a burning town.

Their mouths left bruises, starting with the kiss
and ending with the proverb, where they stayed;
never in making was there brighter bliss,
followed by darker shame. Thus I was made.

Aunt Jane

Aunt Jane, of whom I dreamed the nights it
    thundered,
was dead at ninety, buried at a hundred.
We kept her corpse a decade, hid upstairs,
where it ate porridge, slept and said its prayers.

And every night before I went to bed
they took me in to worship with the dead.
Christ Lord, if I should die before I wake,
I pray thee Lord my body take.

The Belled Deer

There used to be wild deer across the river,
one of them wore a bell and no one knew
its origin and so the legends grew;
grandfather thought no natural brute was ever
as swift as that one was or half so clever.
Though every fall the hunters sought her, told
of bell-sounds like the touch of ice on gold,
they said that mortal hand would kill her never.

Nobody hunts there now; a tracker's snow,
a windless afternoon were once enough
to sweep the orchards with a rifle screen.
They wanted meat, of course, for times were tough,
but there was not a man who had not seen
the belled deer in his sights and let her go.

The Coat

My grandmother's boy is dead,
his skull fractured he did not speak
as she knelt down on the dirt road
and wept on his face, her hand under his head.

My grandmother's boy was wild
as the blackbirds in Minard's clearing.
He stood up on the pedals, yodelling;
the wind too seems to ride toward death.

My father took the corduroy coat
of my grandmother's boy and hid
it behind a beam where she found it and came
weeping with it hugged to her breast,
walking slowly under the clothes line
down the pathway beside the woodshed.

There were bloody stains and the stains of mud
almost indistinguishable on the coat,
and her black dress with its red flowers
came like a ghost berating
my father as though he'd killed.
When he took the coat from her
he was so gentle I was amazed. Afterwards
he cursed and poked the coat viciously,
using a stick to crowd it
into the kitchen fire.

Father

Father, she says, was handsome as a Spaniard,
rode a bay stallion in the Depression
and fed it better than he fed himself.
He was a strict and pious gentleman.

He called me princess even when he paced
his study with the black hypnotic tongue
of the whip licking at his riding boot.
There's not one man like him among the young.

Baptism

In summer-coloured dresses, six young girls
are walking in the river; they look back,
frightened and proud; a choir and a cloud
of starlings sing; in rubber boots and black
frock-coat the preacher bends them separately
under; since the up-rushing stream expands
their skirts as they go down he closes them
each time with gently disapproving hands.

The Fynch Cows

The Fynch cows poisoned:
they'd torn the fence down,
gored one another for the befouled weed;
next day they bloated
and their bowels bled,
and they staggered crazily
around the miserly pasture —

John Fynch crying
as he stumbled after them,
with his rifle.

Warren Pryor

When every pencil meant a sacrifice
his parents boarded him at school in town,
slaving to free him from the stony fields,
the meagre acreage that bore them down.

They blushed with pride when, at his graduation,
they watched him picking up the slender scroll,
his passport from the years of brutal toil
and lonely patience in a barren hole.

When he went in the Bank their cups ran over.
They marvelled how he wore a milk-white shirt
work days and jeans on Sundays. He was saved
from their thistle-strewn farm and its red dirt.

And he said nothing. Hard and serious
like a young bear inside his teller's cage,
his axe-hewn hands upon the paper bills
aching with empty strength and throttled rage.

Georgie and Fenwick

Georgie and Fenwick Cranston,
in their thirties and unmarried,
Hainesville calls them old bachelors,
live with their parents on a potato farm,
six miles north of town —
they're afraid of girls.

> Saturday nights,
> in front of the Farmers Store
> some of the girls,
> their little posteriors
> gift-wrapped in Christmas-coloured
> short pants, always stop
> to tease them.

Cecelia Cameron, pressing
so close to Fenwick his overalls
scratch her bare legs, whispers,
Fenwick, do you still love me?

> When she backs away
> her breasts ripple
> under her striped blouse,
> she puts her fists in her pockets,
> tightening her pants,
> tugging them up her thighs,
> she says, Georgie
> do you want to take me home tonight?

And everybody laughs,
except Georgie and Fenwick,
who say nothing,
their mouths open,

their eyes half-shut,
blushing, rocking back and forth
in their gum rubbers. They look
like rabbits frozen
with fear of the gun.

Christ

Aloft in a balsam fir I watched Christ go,
two crows in that same tree made human laughter.

He clambered over the log fence and crossed
the orange-yellow field, his purple skirts

swishing the grain and I could hear that sound,
so close he was, and separate the hairs

in his red beard. He passed beneath me, never
once looking up, and having reached the gate

to the hill pasture shrank smaller and smaller
becoming first a fist and then a finger

and then a fleck of purple on the hillside.
At last, at the edge of the wood, he vanished
            altogether.

Looking for Nancy

Looking for Nancy
        everywhere, I've stopped
girls in trenchcoats
and blue dresses,
        said
Nancy I've looked
        all over
        hell for you,
Nancy I've been afraid
that I'd die
before I found you.

        But there's always
        been some mistake:

a broken streetlight,
too much rum or merely
my wanting too much
for it to be her.

St. John River

The colour of a bayonet this river
that glitters blue and solid on the page
in tourist folders, yet some thirty towns
use it as a latrine, the sewerage
seeping back to their wells, and farmers maddened
by debt or queer religions winter down
under the ice, the river bottom strewn
with heaps of decomposing bark torn loose
from pulpwood driven south, its acid juice
killing the salmon. August, when the stink
of the corrupted water floats like gas
along these streets, what most astonishes
is that the pictures haven't lied, the real
river is beautiful, as blue as steel.

Party at Bannon Brook

At the dead end of a road twisting snakelike
as that out of Eden, in a hunting camp, the hoarse creek crawling
through the closed door like the wet ghost of some drowned Adam,
coughing water on the floor, I sprawl on a straw-filled bunk
and drink rum with strangers:

> The chef in his tall white hat
> and apron embroidered
> with ribald slogans,
> spears steaks with slivers
> of white pine, roaring.

Beside me, in the leaping shadows
next the rough boards of the wall, her head
resting on a calendar from which all the months
have been ripped away, leaving only
the likeness of a woman
with orange skin and a body that might have been
stretched on a rack in the dungeon
of Gilles de Rais, it has such perverse,
blasphemous proportions, a girl sits, swaying
in time with the chef's song, her sweater
pulled out at the back, my circular arm
stroking the soft fat
of her belly — not because I love her
but because I am afraid. If we could do what we wish,
always, I would tell them I understand:
this is the season
when the bobcat is not driven away
by smoke, and the eagle
makes reconnaissance from the coast.

> But they will not listen.
> And they could do worse: tomorrow

the chef will be cashiered, kill eight hours
sending bills to debtors and this girl
sit at a desk, addressing letters
to the brains of dead men, each a packaged pudding
shelved in cold storage, and I

in whom despair
has bred superior cunning
will escape only by long study
of how the silver beads turn to gold, falling
by my employer's window, the icicles
stroked by an amorous sun.

Disguise

This is the amazing thing
that it is so easy
to fool them —
the sane bastards.

I can talk
about weather, eat,
preside at meetings
of the PTA.
They don't know.

Me foreign as a Martian.
With the third eye in my forehead!
But I comb my hair
cleverly so it doesn't show

except a little
sometimes when the wind blows.

The Bull Moose

Down from the purple mist of trees on the mountain,
lurching through forests of white spruce and cedar,
stumbling through tamarack swamps,
came the bull moose
to be stopped at last by a pole-fenced pasture.

Too tired to turn or, perhaps, aware
there was no place left to go, he stood with the cattle.
They, scenting the musk of death, seeing his great head
like the ritual mask of a blood god, moved to the other end
of the field, and waited.

The neighbours heard of it, and by afternoon
cars lined the road. The children teased him
with alder switches and he gazed at them
like an old, tolerant collie. The women asked
if he could have escaped from a Fair.

The oldest man in the parish remembered seeing
a gelded moose yoked with an ox for plowing.
The young men snickered and tried to pour beer
down his throat, while their girl friends took their pictures.

And the bull moose let them stroke his tick-ravaged flanks,
let them pry open his jaws with bottles, let a giggling girl
plant a little purple cap
of thistles on his head.

When the wardens came, everyone agreed it was a shame
to shoot anything so shaggy and cuddlesome.
He looked like the kind of pet
women put to bed with their sons.

So they held their fire. But just as the sun dropped in the river
the bull moose gathered his strength
like a scaffolded king, straightened and lifted his horns
so that even the wardens backed away as they raised their rifles.
When he roared, people ran to their cars. All the young men
leaned on their automobile horns as he toppled.

The Shack Dwellers

Most of them look
as though their bodies were boneless.

Every animal
has its own defense:
theirs is plasticity.

Kick them in the face
and nothing breaks.
It's as if your boot
sank in wet dough.

But sometimes a trick
of hunger or heredity
gives one small bones
like an aristocrat's,
transparent skin
and delicate, blue veins.

You'll see one of the lost
Bourbons or Romanoffs,
dirty toes protruding
from the holes in his sneakers,
a hint of the old
hauteur in his hawk nose
as he tries to talk the grocer
out of a roll of bologna
and a loaf of stale bread.

Stoney Ridge Dance Hall

They don't like strangers.
So be careful how you smile.

Eight generations
of Hungerfords, McGards and Staceys
have lived on this ridge
like incestuous kings.
Their blood is so pure
it will not clot.

This is the only
country they know.
There are men here
who have never heard of Canada.

When they tire of dancing
they go down the road
and drink white lightning
out of the bung
of a molasses puncheon.

But they never forget
to strap on the knuckles
they've made from beer bottle
caps and leather

and there are sharp spikes
in their orange logging boots.

The Grove Beyond the Barley

This grove is too secret: one thinks of murder.
Coming upon your white body (for as yet
I do not know you, therefore have no right
to speak of discovering
you, can address myself
to your body only) seeing the disorder
of your naked limbs, the arms outstretched
like one crucified, the legs bent like a runner's,
it took me less than a second to write a novel:
the husband in the black suit
worn at his wedding, the hired man
in his shirt the colour
of a rooster's comb and, in the end, you
thrown here like an axed colt.
Then I saw your breasts: they are not asleep,
move like the shadows of leaves
stirred by the wind. I hope you do not waken,
before I go; one who chooses
so dark a place
to lie naked
might cry out. The shadows quicken,
I wish you a lover,
dreams of sunlit meadows,
imagine myself a gentle satyr.

The Execution

On the night of the execution
a man at the door
mistook me for the coroner.
"Press," I said.

But he didn't understand. He led me
into the wrong room
where the sheriff greeted me:
"You're late, Padre."

"You're wrong," I told him. "I'm Press."
"Yes, of course, Reverend Press."
We went down a stairway.

"Ah, Mr. Ellis," said the Deputy.
"Press!" I shouted. But he shoved me
through a black curtain.
The lights were so bright
I couldn't see the faces
of the men sitting
opposite. But, thank God, I thought
they can see me!

"Look!" I cried. "Look at my face!
Doesn't anybody know me?"

Then a hood covered my head.
"Don't make it harder for us," the hangman whispered.

The Drunken Poet

Sometimes, when he got drunk and came back late,
he stopped a moment before every door
in the dark hallway of the boarding house,
like an intrusive saint, or murderer.

And he knew everything that those within
slept with, they laughed and whimpered in their sleep,
and he had half a mind to blackmail them
and half a mind to cover them and weep.

Later, in his own room, he seized a pen
and paper, set down everything he knew,
and re-united God and devil, since
he shared all secrets common to the two.

Each time he laughed he tasted salt. Each tear
tickled him still he howled. He went to bed,
the papers in his hand, awoke too sick
to go to work and burned them all, unread.

Daisies

We walked a mile from the road, and with every step
she broke off a daisy, till she held thousands
in a great bunch against her chest,

till they covered her face and her red-gold pigtails,
till the top of her head was the eye of a daisy;
she sniffed of them, tasted their petals and pulp,
felt their heads and stalks with her cheeks and fingers.

That soil was rich, had we walked all day
she could have kept counting her steps with daisies:
running back to the car, she threw open her arms
and her body burst like a fountain of flowers.

Canadian Love Song

Your body's a small word with many meanings.
Love. If. Yes. But. Death.
Surely I will love you a little while,
perhaps as long as I have breath.

December is thirteen months long,
July's one afternoon; therefore,
lovers must outwit wool,
learn how to puncture fur.

To my love's bed, to keep her warm,
I'll carry wrapped and heated stones.
That which is comfort to the flesh
is sometimes torture to the bones.

The Migrant Hand

For how many thousands of years, for how many millions
of baskets and waggonloads and truckloads of onions,
or cotton, or turnips has this old man knelt
in the dirt of sun-crazy fields? If you ask him,
he'll put you off: he's suspicious of questions.
The truth is that Adam, a day out of Eden,
started him gathering grapes: old Pharaoh
sold him to Greece; he picked leeks for the Seljuks,
garlic for Tuscans, Goths and Normans,
pumpkins and maize for the Pilgrim Fathers,
has forgotten them all, forgotten all of the past, except
the last ten hours of blackflies and heat,
the last two hundred barrels of potatoes.

I, Icarus

There was a time when I could fly. I swear it.
Perhaps, if I think hard for a moment, I can even tell you the year.
My room was on the ground floor at the rear of the house.
My bed faced a window.
Night after night I lay on my bed and willed myself to fly.
It was hard work, I can tell you.
Sometimes I lay perfectly still for an hour before I felt
    my body rising from the bed.
I rose slowly, slowly until I floated three or four feet
    above the floor.
Then, with a kind of swimming motion, I propelled myself
    toward the window.
Outside, I rose higher and higher, above the pasture fence,
    above the clothesline, above the dark, haunted trees
    beyond the pasture.
And, all the time, I heard the music of flutes.
It seemed the wind made this music.
And sometimes there were voices singing.

Long, Long Ago

It seems I always saw the Indian woman
the instant she became visible,
and never took my eyes off her
as she lugged her many-coloured pack,
three times as big as herself,
down South Mountain,
across the Little Bridge,
up North Mountain
and into our kitchen
where she undid a knot
and flooded the entire room with baskets
— cherry-coloured baskets,
cabbage-coloured baskets,
baskets the colour of a November sky,
each basket containing
another, smaller basket,
down to one so tiny it would hold
only a hang of thread and a thimble.

And He Wept Aloud, So That the Egyptians Heard It

In my grandfather's house
for the first time in years,
houseflies big as bumblebees
playing crazy football
in the skim-milk-coloured windows,

leap-frogging from
the cracked butter saucer
to our tin plates of
rainbow trout and potatoes, catching the bread
on its way to our mouths,
        mounting one another
        on the rough deal table.

It was not so much their filth
as their numbers and persistence and —
oh, admit this, man, there's no point in poetry
if you withhold the truth
once you've come by it —
        their symbolism:
        Baal-Zebub,
god of the poor and outcast,

that enraged me, made me snatch the old man's
Family Herald, attack them like a maniac,
lay to left and right until the window sills
over-flowed with their smashed corpses,
until bits of their wings
stuck to my fingers,
until the room buzzed with their terror . . .

And my grandfather, bewildered and afraid,
came to help me:
    "never seen a year
    when the flies were so thick"
as though he'd seen them at all before I came!

His voice so old and baffled and pitiful
that I threw my club into the wood box and sat down
    and wanted to beg his forgiveness
as we ate on in silence broken only
by the almost inaudible humming
of the flies rebuilding their world.

Daughter of Zion

Seeing the bloodless lips, the ugly knot of salt-coloured hair,
the shapeless housedress with its grotesque flowers
like those printed on the wallpaper in cheap rooming houses,
sadder than if she wore black,

observing how she tries to avoid the sun,
crossing the street with eyes cast down
as though such fierce light were an indecent spectacle:
if darkness could be bought like yard goods
she would stuff her shopping bag with shadows,

noting all this and more,
who would look at her twice?
What stranger would suspect that only last night
in a tent by the river,
in the aisles between the rows
of rough planks laid on kitchen chairs,
before an altar of orange crates,
in the light of a kerosene lantern,
God Himself, the Old One, seized her in his arms and lifted
    her up and danced with her,
and Christ, with the sawdust clinging to his garments and
    the sweat of the carpenter's shop
on his body and the smell of wine and garlic on his breath,
drew her to his breast and kissed her,

and the Holy Ghost
went into her body and spoke through her mouth
the language they speak in heaven!

Britain Street

Saint John, New Brunswick

This is a street at war.
The smallest children
battle with clubs
till the blood comes,
shout "fuck you!"
like a rallying cry —

while mothers shriek
from doorsteps and windows
as though the very names
of their young were curses:

"Brian! Marlene!
Damn you! God damn you!"

or waddle into the street
to beat their own with switches:
"I'll teach you, Brian!
I'll teach you, God damn you!"

On this street,
even the dogs
would rather fight
than eat.

I have lived here nine months
and in all that time
have never once heard
a gentle word spoken.

I like to tell myself
that is only because
gentle words are whispered
and harsh words shouted.

For Jean Vincent D'Abbadie, Baron St.-Castin

Take heart, monsieur, four-fifths of this province
is still much as you left it: forest, swamp and barren.
Even now, after three hundred years, your enemies
    fear ambush, huddle by coasts and rivers,
the dark woods at their backs.

    Oh, you'd laugh to see
how old Increase Mather and his ghastly Calvinists
patrol the palisades, how they bury their money
under the floors of their hideous churches
lest you come again in the night
with the red ochre mark of the sun god
on your forehead, you exile from the Pyrenees,
    you baron of France and Navarre,
you squaw man, you Latin poet,
    you war chief of Penobscot
and of Kennebec and of Maliseet!

    At the winter solstice
your enemies cry out in their sleep
and the great trees throw back their heads and shout
    nabujcol!
Take heart, monsieur,
even the premier, even the archbishop,
even the poor gnome-like slaves
at the all-night diner and the service station
will hear you chant
    The Song of Roland
as you cross yourself
and reach for your scalping knife.

July 15

The wind is cool. Nothing is happening.
I do not strive for meaning. When I lie on my back
the wind passes over me, I do not feel it.
The sun has hands
like a woman, calling the heat
out of my body.
The trees sing. Nothing is happening.

When I close my eyes,
I hear the soft footsteps
of the grass. Nothing is happening.

How long have I lain here?
Well, it is still summer. But is it the same
summer I came?
I must remember
not to ask myself questions.
I am naked. Trees sing. The grass walks.
Nothing is happening.

A Mug's Game

At the party that followed the poetry reading,
one girl kept telling me how thrilled she was to meet
someone who hadn't gone to university, and another said
I reminded her so much of whoever it was who played
in *Bus Stop* she kept expecting Marilyn to walk in, and the hostess
extending three bite-size salami sandwiches
and a glass of warm whiskey and ginger ale
smiled at me like Li'l Abner's Aunt Bessie
welcoming her nephew to Toronto.

The man from the CBC, who said: "Of course, you're staying
at the YMCA" and thought he was humouring me
by acting impressed when he found out I wasn't,

explained: "The purpose of such readings is to give writers
from unlikely places like Hartland, New Brunswick,
the chance to communicate
with others
of their own kind."

The Word

Though I have the gift of tongues
and can move mountains,
my words are nothing
compared with yours,
though you only
look up from my arms
and whisper my name.

This is not pride
because I know
it is not
my name that you whisper
but a sign
between us,
like the word
that was spoken
at the beginning
of the world
and will be spoken again
only when the world ends.

This is not that word
but the other
that must be spoken
over and over
while the world lasts.

Tears,
laughter,
a lifetime!
All in one word!

The word you whisper
when you look up
from my arms
and seem to say
my name.

Day's End
for Anne

I have worked since daylight in the hayfields.
We walked home at dusk, following the horses.
For supper, I ate hot bread and spiced ham,
    onions and tomatoes.
Now I kneel over a basin of cold water
and a woman washes my hair —
a strong woman whose knuckles rake my scalp.
Her hands smell of soap, I am naked to the waist,
    she leans her weight against me;
laughs huskily when I seize her wrists
    and try to push away her hands.
I am young and strong but a great weariness is upon me —
I would be willing to die now if I were sure that death is sleep.

The Last Waltz

The orchestra playing
the last waltz
at three o'clock
in the morning
in the Knights of Pythias Hall
in Hartland, New Brunswick,
Canada, North America,
world, solar system,
centre of the universe —

and all of us drunk,
swaying together
to the music of rum
and a sad clarinet:

comrades all,
each with his beloved.

The Wickedness of Peter Shannon

Peter had experienced the tight, nauseous desire
to be swallowed up by the earth, to have his blue
eyes plucked out of his fourteen-year-old head,
his arms sliced off, himself dismembered and the
remnants hidden forever, his shame was so unanswerable.
Oh, God, God, God, it was so he could take any part
of Nancy Lynn O'Mally and lie open-eyed and stark
in the darkness with it — her lilting backsides
in the candy-cane shorts — and bring his thighs together
like pliers, muttering, and it was like the taste
of peach ice cream and the smoke of leaves burning
and the wanton savagery of a pillow over his face,
breaking him, until he swung out over the seething
water and the limb went down and down and down and
the rain was a thousand horses urinating on the
fireproof shingles and he whispered . . . ohhhhhh,
Jesussss . . . mad as a turpentined colt among the rockpiles
in the north pasture; what are your breasts like
Nancy Lynn O'Mally, how is it that no matter how much
I'm ashamed I don't blush, except in company . . . my cheeks
burning as though Christ slapped them!

In the Operating Room

The anesthetist is singing
"Michael, row the boat ashore,
Hallelujah!"
And I am astonished
that his arms
are so hairy —
thick, red, curly hair
like little coppery ferns
growing out of
his flesh
from wrist
to shoulder.
I would like
to reach up
and touch
the hairy arm
of the anesthetist
because it may be
the last living thing
I will ever see
and I am glad
it is not
white and hairless
— but if I reached up
and wound
a few wisps
of his hair
around my forefinger
as I would like to do
they would think
their drugs
had made me silly
and might remember

and laugh
if I live,
so I concentrate
very hard
on the song
the anesthetist
is singing —
"The River Jordan
is muddy and cold,
Hallelujah!"
And soon
everything
is dark
and nothing
matters
and when I try
to reach up
and touch
the hair
which I think of
now as
little jets
of fire,
I discover
they've strapped
my arms
to the table.

Morning of the Third Operation

Thinking,
just as I
blacked out:
what if all
the evidence
is wrong,
what if
the dead
look on
but can't
make us
understand,
what if
I die
and go home
and Claudine
is crying:
will she know
what it means
even if I
have the strength
to knock
a pencil
off the table.
Listen, Claudine,
look at me!
I'm alive!
Don't be
so damned
stupid, woman.
I'm here
beside you.
But she keeps on

crying
and then
a friend comes
and takes her away
because it isn't good
for her
to be alone.

The Mysterious Naked Man

A mysterious naked man has been reported
on Cranston Avenue. The police are performing
the usual ceremonies with coloured lights and sirens.
Almost everyone is outdoors and strangers are conversing
    excitedly
as they do during disasters when their involvement is
    peripheral.
"What did he look like?" the lieutenant is asking.
"I don't know," says the witness. "He was naked."
There is talk of dogs — this is no ordinary case
of indecent exposure, the man has been seen
a dozen times since the milkman spotted him and now
the sky is turning purple and voices
carry a long way and the children
have gone a little crazy as they often do at dusk
and cars are arriving
from other sections of the city.
And the mysterious naked man
is kneeling behind a garbage can or lying on his belly
in somebody's garden
or maybe even hiding in the branches of a tree,
where the wind from the harbour
whips at his naked body,
and by now he's probably done
whatever it was he wanted to do
and wishes he could go to sleep
or die
or take to the air like Superman.

Hymn to Dionysus

The trick is to loose
    the wild bear
        but hold tight
to the chain,
    woe
        when the bear
snatches up
    the links
        and the man dances.

Country Full of Christmas

Country full of Christmas,
the stripped, suspicious elms
groping for the dun sky —
what can I give my love?

The remembrance — mouse hawks
scudding on the dykes, above
the wild roses; horses and cattle
separate in the same field.
It is not for my love.

Do you know that foxes
believe in nothing
but themselves — everything
is a fox disguised: men, dogs and rabbits.

Snapshot

It takes even more than this to make you cry
or laugh
    aloud
        when you are old enough
to find a forgotten snapshot of yourself,

take it up in your hands,
hold it close to the light,

discover slowly
    and for the first time

that once
    long ago
        you were almost

beautiful.

The Mosherville Road

If a man wishes to be sure
of the road he treads on, he
must close his eyes and walk
in the dark.

St. John of the Cross

It is nowhere so dark
    as in the country
        where I was born.
I remember nights
    I held my hand
        an inch from my eyes
and saw nothing.
    Yet I kept putting one
        foot in front of the other
and don't recall ever falling
    into the ditch,
        though I was so aware
of it, three feet deep,
    on both sides of me
        with gravel walls
and filthy water
    at the bottom of it,
        that it seems to me now
I must have gone into it,
    at least once
        and forgotten. There was glass
from broken bottles
    and everything else
        that gets thrown from cars
in that ditch and thorn bushes grew
    on the opposite side of it,
        and there were trees

and night birds
    and flying insects
        I couldn't see.
Usually I talked
    to myself and sometimes I sang
        as I stumbled along
and it wasn't until tonight
    almost twenty years
        later I began to realize
how much I was afraid.

A Poem About Miracles

Why don't records go blank
the instant the singer dies?
Oh, I know there are explanations,
but they don't convince me.
I'm still surprised
when I hear the dead singing.
As for orchestras,
I expect the instruments
to fall silent one by one
as the musicians succumb
to cancer and heart disease
so that toward the end
I turn on a disc
labelled *Götterdämmerung*
and all that comes out
is the sound of one sick old man
scraping a shaky bow
across an out-of-tune fiddle.

Ypres: 1915

The age of trumpets is passed, the banners hang
like dead crows, tattered and black,
rotting into nothingness on cathedral walls.
In the crypt of St. Paul's I had all the wrong thoughts,
wondered if there was anything left of Nelson
or Wellington, and even wished
I could pry open their tombs and look,
then was ashamed
of such morbid childishness, and almost afraid.

I know the picture is as much a forgery
as the Protocols of Zion, yet it outdistances
more plausible fictions: newsreels, regimental histories,
biographies of Earl Haig.
                              It is always morning
and the sky somehow manages to be red
though the picture is in black and white.
There is a long road over flat country,
shell holes, the debris of houses,
a gun carriage overturned in a field,
the bodies of men and horses,
but only a few of them and those
always neat and distant.
                              The Moors are running
down the right side of the road.
The Moors are running
in their baggy pants and Santa Claus caps.
The Moors are running.
                              And their officers,
Frenchmen who remember
Alsace and Lorraine,
are running backwards in front of them,
waving their swords, trying to drive them back,

weeping
        at the dishonour of it all.
The Moors are running.

And on the left side of the same road,
the Canadians are marching
in the opposite direction.

The Canadians are marching
in English uniforms behind
a piper playing "Scotland the Brave."

The Canadians are marching
in impeccable formation,
every man in step.

The Canadians are marching.

And I know this belongs
with Lord Kitchener's moustache
and old movies in which the Kaiser and his general staff
seem to run like the Keystone Cops.

That old man on television last night,
a farmer or fisherman by the sound of him,
revisiting Vimy Ridge, and they asked him
what it was like, and he said,
There was water up to our middles, yes
and there was rats, and yes
there was water up to our middles
and rats, all right enough,
and to tell you the truth
after the first three or four days
I started to get a little disgusted.

Oh, I know they were mercenaries
in a war that hardly concerned us.
I know all that.

Sometimes I'm not even sure that I have a country.

But I know they stood there at Ypres
the first time the Germans used gas,
that they were almost the only troops
in that section of the front
who did not break and run,
who held the line.

Perhaps they were too scared to run.
Perhaps they didn't know any better
— that is possible, they were so innocent,
those farmboys and mechanics, you have only to look
at old pictures and see how they smiled.
Perhaps they were too shy
to walk out on anybody, even Death.
Perhaps their only motivation
was a stubborn disinclination.

Private MacNally thinking:
You squareheaded sons of bitches,
you want this God damn trench
you're going to have to take it away
from Billy MacNally
of the South End of Saint John, New Brunswick.

And that's ridiculous, too, and nothing
on which to found a country.
                              Still
It makes me feel good, knowing
that in some obscure, conclusive way
they were connected with me
and me with them.

A Black Plastic Button and a Yellow Yoyo

I wish I could make her understand
her child isn't the Christ Child
and didn't create the world,
then maybe she'd stop shaking
her fists in his face
and he could come out from inside
his yellow yoyo
or black plastic button
because that's where he hides:
I've watched from my window,
unable to write because of her screaming,
and seen him flying out of his body
into the yoyo,
where he can neither see nor be seen,
neither hear nor speak,
a Buddha smaller than my thumb,
a sleeping Krishna,
there inside that dancing yoyo;
and if she knocks it from his hand,
why, he simply turns
the second button from the top
of his windbreaker,
a black plastic button,
turns it between
his thumb and forefinger,
focuses his eyes on it,
until he is safe again,
curled up in a ball
where nothing at all can reach him.

The First Stirring of the Beasts

The first stirring of the beasts
is heard at two or three or four
in the morning, depending on the season.

You lie, warm and drowsy, listening,
wondering how there is so much difference
between the sounds
cattle and horses make,
moving in their stanchions or halters,
so much difference that you can't explain,
so that if someone asked you
which of them is moving now?
you couldn't answer
but lying there, not quite awake,
you know, although it doesn't matter,
and then a rooster crows
and it sounds, or maybe you imagine this,
unsure and a little afraid,
                              and after a little
there are only the sounds of night
that we call silence.

The second stirring of the beasts
is the one everybody understands.
You hear it at dawn
and if you belong here
you get up.
Anyway, there is no mystery
in it, it is the other stirring,
the first brief restlessness
which seems to come for no reason
that makes you ask yourself
what are they awake for?

An Exchange of Gifts

As long as you read this poem
I will be writing it.
I am writing it here and now
before your eyes,
although you can't see me.
Perhaps you'll dismiss this
as a verbal trick,
the joke is you're wrong;
the real trick
is your pretending
this is something
fixed and solid,
external to us both.
I tell you better:
I will keep on
writing this poem for you
even after I'm dead.

Chance Encounter

There is something odd in the road ahead.
A man in a black coat walking a dog,
a tall man in a long black coat walking a big red dog,
or is it a black mare with a red colt.
                              God
don't let me hit them.
                         I don't like
to be splashed by death.
                         The car stops in time
and I roll down the window.
                              There is a cow moose
standing not ten feet away
and her calf a little farther off,
neither of them knowing what to make of the headlights,
bright as lightning, solid as the light
of a full moon on a cloudless night.
Then the cow crosses over, very slowly,
not looking back
until she reaches
the edge of the woods
on the other side
and finds the calf has not followed her,
                                   but gone back
and they look at one another
across the light that separates them
and perhaps she makes little coaxing sounds I can't hear,
while I will him
not to run away where they might never find each other
but to be brave enough
to walk into the light
I don't dare turn off
for fear of humans like myself
— and at last he begins to walk

toward the road
                        and after a moment's pause
enters the light
                    and crosses it
in about thirty seconds,
                              a long time
when you're holding your breath,
                                        and the instant
he's safely over, she runs and he
        runs behind her,
                and I drive on,
                            happy about it all,
bursting to tell someone about the great sight I've seen,
yet not even sure why it should seem so important.

Why He Wanted to Abolish Capital Punishment

When I was a boy I imagined
I was motivated by my
extraordinary compassion.
As a youth I laughed and said:
"I suppose the real reason is
I'm scared they'll get *me*."
Then I became a man and discovered
I'd always been afraid
if it didn't end
there'd come a time
when I wouldn't be able
to stop myself:
one day I'd have to go down and tell them
to forget about the fee,
I'd be hangman for nothing,
just for the fun of it,
if they'd let me.

Mistaken Identity

It's good sometimes
to be mistaken for
someone else, although
it usually ends
badly.
        Getting down from
a bus in Boston
in 1951, when I was
seventeen, I stepped
into the arms of
a fat woman whose
breath smelled of
beer, and she kissed
me on the mouth and
said, Walter, Walter,
and I was so lonesome
that for a second I
was almost tempted
to pass myself
off as whoever she
thought I was; but
what I did was
mumble something
about there being
a mistake, and even
before I spoke she
had realized that
and was pushing
me away.
        Another time
a beautiful young girl
blew a kiss at me
from the open window

72

of a cab in New Haven,
Connecticut, and
shouted, Hi, Davie!
She wore a red scarf,
I remember. And I waved.
Then because I wanted
her to keep smiling
at me, lovingly, I
very quickly
turned away.

Fair Warning

I keep a lunatic chained
to a beam in the attic. He
is my twin brother whom
I'm trying to cheat
out of his inheritance.
It's all right for me
to tell you this because
you won't believe it.
Nobody believes anything
that's put in a poem.
I could confess to
murder and as long as
I did it in a verse
there's not a court
that would convict me.
So if you're ever
a guest overnight
in my house, don't
go looking for
the source of any
unusual sounds.

The Iconotrophic Instant
for Robert Cockburn

The old remember everything:
nothing is lost.
                If your lover outlives you
by half a century and when asked your name
cannot recall it, names are less important
than your falling in the snow that night,
near a bonfire or under a neon light,
and rolling in it like a child
though you were already
the mother of his children.
He never tires of telling it:
"Once, I remember, she slipped
on an ice patch, fell down and rolled over and over
like a kitten or a puppy."
Those who care for his needs
wink at one another, they do not know
he has told them the whole story
of his love for you, of your love for him.
And that old soldier
in the hundred-year-old diary
of an English curate:
                Talking of wolves,
he said he remembered,
how every night they came down to drink from the river,
four or five of them, like mastiffs and as big.
The soldiers used to scare them
by snapping the locks
of their flint muskets, making the powder flash.
When the wolves saw it they went away.
They did not like to see that.
"It is nothing to write," the curate wrote,
yet he was wise enough

to record it twice in five months
during which he must have heard it
scores of times.
        It was one man's history
of the Peninsular men who followed hook-nosed Atty,
not yet Wellington, into Portugal, through Spain,
    across the Pyrenees.

Canadian January Night

Ice storm: the hill
a pyramid of black crystal
down which the cars
slide like phosphorescent beetles
while I, walking backwards in obedience
to the wind, am possessed
of the fearful knowledge
my compatriots share
but almost never utter:
this is a country
where a man can die
                    simply from being
caught outside.

The Married Man's Poem

Five years married
and he has never once
wished he dared kill her,
                    which means
they're happy enough.
But it isn't love.

He Raids the Refrigerator and Reflects on Parenthood

Nowlan, you maudlin boob,
almost blubbering because
two hours ago at the party
your son said, I'll be
fifteen tomorrow, can I
have a whole pint of beer?
Grinning so he could say
it was a joke if you
took it that way; but he
was serious all right:
it's like music sometimes
how serious he can be
about small matters
which you're thereby
reminded were
important.
      And you hesitated,
not because you ever
considered refusing
but because you wanted him
to know that you, too,
value rituals. But
there were only enough
cool ones for the guests.
So you gave him a warm one.
It doesn't matter, he said.
It's okay. But of course it did.
The rite was spoiled
by an imperfection. And now he's
asleep upstairs and you're
holding open the door
of the refrigerator, contemplating

a pint bottle with no more
than two ounces taken from it
and the cap put back so well
you'd need an opener
to take it off again, thinking
of the petty treason
we commit so often
against those we love,
the confidence games
in which parents play
their children for suckers.

Johnnie's Poem

Look! I've written a poem!
Johnnie says
and hands it to me
        and it's about
        his grandfather dying
        last summer, and me
        in the hospital
and I want to cry,
don't you see, because it doesn't matter
if it's not very good:
        what matters is he knows
and it was me, his father, who told him
        you write poems about what
        you feel deepest and hardest.

Cornflowers

I am a saint with a broken wing
      who shakes his fists like the wind.
                                 You
are the homecoming
           of the sun,
                  an hurrah of grass.
The cornflowers are not yet
      aware they will die soon
            from last night's frost.
They are like the Empress
Elizabeth of Austria
who was stabbed with a blade so thin
she continued to smile
                 and did not interrupt
her walk,
        although it had pierced her heart.
Since in this place and season
      they are the only flowers
           that do not ask for money
I give you them.
        Nothing else is beautiful
this hunchbacked October night
except the moon.

Written While Waiting for Another Chest X-Ray

I don't want to die.
That sounds like something said
by one of the more stupid
19th century kings, some Maximilian or Ferdinand
who in his youth admired Byron
and nibbled the ears
of the prettier page boys, in middle age
turned to brandy and took communion
every morning of his life,
grew enormously fat and
in his sixtieth year
summoned a cardinal, said, Your Eminence,
I don't want to die, see that the matter
is taken care of,
                    and with that
went shooting grouse
and killed more than one hundred,
being a most excellent shot.

For Yukio Mishima

> ". . . The novelist, often men-
> tioned as a possible Nobel Prize
> winner, stripped to his waist,
> unbuttoned his trousers and
> sat down on the floor of the
> room. He touched his stomach,
> gave a piercing yell and drove
> his short samurai sword into
> himself . . ."   — News Item

You can't hear me, Yukio Mishima. But, then,
a man who addresses the dead is bound to discover,
sooner or later, that he's talking to himself.
The newspapers argue whether
you were certifiably insane
or a buffoon for whom suicide
was the only bit of egocentricity
that remained untasted.
They can't find words for you
as they could so readily have done
if you'd decapitated yourself
while driving a racing car
or in any other equally extravagant
but fashionable manner;
just as they couldn't admit
it was a bull that got Hemingway:
there were hoofprints leading away
from the lodge where his body lay
and a trail of blood
that had dripped from the horns.
That was never published.
But perhaps I understand you better than most,
Yukio Mishima, wanting to restore the sword

to its place beside the chrysanthemums.
The worst way to die
is as a prisoner, at the hands
of a pitiless human enemy.
                              Next to the worst
is death of natural causes.
There are no pacifists
in the cancer ward.
                    That great war chief
whose people called him *Our Strange Man*
and whom the whites called Crazy Horse,
led his soldiers into battle shouting:
"Come on, Lakota, it's a good day to die!"
My grandfather left
an imitation leather cardboard wallet
containing a Junior G-Man secret pocket,
five greenish pennies, and a will beginning:
"I, Cathal O Nuallain, Prince of Fortara. . . ."
Myself, delirious, coming out from under
the ether and into the demerol
like a man crawling out of the sea
and into the jungle,
resolved to die like
an Irish prince: an old man's foolishness,
a small boy's games
dignifying the fear, almost
sanctifying the pain.

Old Town Revisited

I will park on the corner in front
of the furniture store. The day I left
eight years ago, Moses Timmins stood
across the street, on the top step
to the post office. He waved goodbye.
When I went back
for the first time, a year
later, I found he had descended
only one step (there are five)
and was still waving. I'm
telling you the truth. He had moved
less than a foot in twelve months.
This morning, though, he should be
about to put his foot on the sidewalk.
And Henry Ferguson may have finished
closing the door of The Dough Boy Diner
— he was about to touch
the inside handle eight years ago,
and last summer he was almost
outside, but had paused to say
a final word to Mary-Beth MacGuire,
who when I see her next will be washing
the mug she was starting to fill
in 1963 for Standish Morehouse who will
be getting up from his stool to go back
to the office — how many years
I wonder will it take him
to walk that hundred yards? I foresee
myself an old man on his last visit,
leaning on the shoulder of a grown
grandson who may not even be born
twenty years from now, the pair of us
getting out at this same corner. I foresee

Moses, Standish and Henry finally
come near enough to resume
whatever conversations my
first departure interrupted.

They Go Off to Seek Their Fortunes

> *"The three largest*
> *immigrant colonies in*
> *Toronto consist of the*
> *Italians, the Portuguese*
> *and the Maritimers."*
> — *A Torontonian in conversation*

They have their pictures taken, peering at maps.
They stop along the road to buy beer, opening
the bottles in ways peculiar to them:
the tough one uses his teeth, the cool one his belt buckle,
the mouth organ player takes a bottle in each hand,
hooks the caps together and pulls
so that only one comes off.
                    They tell strangers
where they're from and where they're going and how much
their second cousins make in Sudbury. They say,
"I'm from the island," or "I'm from the bay,"
as if there were only one of each in the world.
They wear white socks and copper bracelets.
They light matches on their thumbnails.
                              They spit.
When they're happy they whoop and when they're sad
they can be dangerous. They're almost never
neutral toward anyone — they either like you
or are prepared quite simply to kick
the living Jesus out of you.
                    They are warriors
for whom it's natural to bid goodbye
with a kind of mock military salute.
                         They greet one another
with a meaningful movement that is part

bow, part shrug, part nod, accompanied
by a slight pursing of the lips,
the barest suggestion of a wink.

For My Grandchildren, as Yet Unborn

For my grandchildren
who will never know
the beasts of the fields:
my own grandmother
would call from the pasture
gate, "So-Boss! So-Boss!"
It would be dusk, and the cattle
a half-mile away in the trees,
but Old Mother Whitehead,
leader of the cows, would hear her
and come with the others behind her,
not that she cared
whether they followed,
she alone among them
went where she pleased.
Creeters, my grandmother said,
which meant *creatures* which meant *cows*.
And they'd walk not at all
as they'd walked that morning;
they'd come slowly,
slowly, but not stopping;
it was even
a little frightening
the way they came
out of the woods
and down the hill,
so purposeful they seemed,
Old Mother leading them.

He Takes His Leave

It was as if I'd opened
Grimms' Fairy Tales and lowered myself into
one of the illustrations, become
the stripling taking his leave
of his village, on foot, with a rucksack
containing his other shirt, except I
carried a black cardboard suitcase
and boarded the train, after walking
only two miles: it didn't stop there
unless you raised a flag or,
to be more accurate, fetched from
the waiting room a broomstick
to which a green and grey rag had been
tacked, stood on tiptoe and
shoved it in a rusty iron socket.
The road was muddier
than I had ever seen it
that March day in 1952; I sank
to my ankles, once or twice it
sucked off my shoe.
An old woman emptying slops
called after me, said that she'd pray for me.
Her name was Lilah.
I patted the head
of a half-wild dog.
The wind smelled of sea-salt and sawdust.
I pause at this point to ask
myself if this matters to anyone,
including its author, and decide
at last that it must, if for no other reason
than this: now, nineteen years later,
I sometimes have nightmares in which
it's that same day, but the train

doesn't stop, all the roads are flooded
or blocked with snow, and even
the telephone lines are down,
or, more mysteriously,
the village has been transformed
into an island and there will never be
another boat to the mainland.
When I wake up
the pillow is damp with sweat,
my hands are shaking.

At a Distance He Observes an Unknown Girl
Picking Flowers

If I think hard enough
of the roses and the girl
breaking them off,
of how the flowers would
smell if I touched them, taste if
I were a child again,
if I remember clearly
how the pain of a thorn differs
from other kinds (it's a little
like learning you've been
the victim of a small
disloyalty), if I convince myself
the girl is somebody
I've known well: Catherine
with whom I used to
bicycle to the Pratt
Farm, the pair of us
in bathing suits; I told her
about alewives, called
gaspereaux there, how we'd shipped them
south, salted, in barrels, more than
a century before, food
for slaves — convinced that
the knowledge made both
the fish and us
more important, a part
of what happened
in books; another time
we were stealing apples and I
mistook her ankle for a branch
of the tree, it was so dark, and
we fell to the ground together, young enough

that the pain of it only
excited us, that and the way
it was replaced slowly, by
the realization that
the entire length of
our bodies touched,
which was like being thrown
into cold water and afterwards
drying off in the sun —
if I think hard enough it will appear
I've drawn something out
of the air, my mind pulling
invisible particles
together, forming a mass,
making.

The Palomino Stallion

Though the barn is so warm
that the oats in his manger,
the straw in his bed
seem to give off smoke —

though the wind is so cold,
the snow in the pasture
so deep he'd fall down
and freeze in an hour —

the eleven-month-old
palomino stallion
has gone almost crazy
fighting and pleading
to be let out.

The Social Worker's Poem

"You know them better," said the girl,
whose face glowed with benevolence as from
too much cosmetics, speaking of the poor.
"What can you tell me that might help?"
She planned to do summer social work in a slum.

Do it as a bribe to God, I answered.
Do it because you hate
morons and dirty underwear. Do it because
you are one of those a sense of power causes
to breathe deeply and exhale aloud as if
it were a richer oxygen. Do it to cure
or satisfy some obscure sexual deviation.

But, above all, I said, don't act
from a desire to be loved. Don't ask
so great a payment for your services.
You'll wind up as bitter as the corner grocer
who gave too much credit and went bankrupt.

And remember, Miss, your admonishments
they'll find as irksome as
you're finding these of mine

Take my word for it. They're human.
Most of them will hate you.

The Old Gentleman

If you want to ask
a question, the chairman said,
begin by giving us
your name and address.

So the old gentleman
seated near the back
of the auditorium,
when it came his turn, said
he was Louis St. Laurent
and came from Quebec;

and we all of us laughed:
because that's who he was
and it was the kind of little joke
one expected of an elderly
former prime minister;

but the next time
he said the same thing

and the time after that,
said it quite simply

and it became obvious
it wasn't meant to be funny,

wasn't meant to be anything
other than courteous,

like his holding open the door
for whoever happened to reach it
at the same time he did

and never lighting a cigarette
without offering the pack to
the person in front and the person behind
and the persons seated
on either side of him.

Unfinished Poem

Bring me black slippers.
The corpse would dance.

Poem for Barbara and Lindsay's Wedding

If, three-quarters of a century from here,
a certain woman looking for something else
among old, dusty, half-remembered things,
should happen upon the photograph of you taken
tonight, she might show it to her daughter
and say to her:
                    Look at your great-grandparents
the day they were married; what funny old cameras
they had and what funny old tables and chairs,
and how funny the young men looked
with those big moustaches and their hair
down to their shoulders!
                    And they might laugh
a little at you and by implication at the rest
of us minor historical figures
who went about in clownish costumes
uttering quaint expressions.
                    But then
if there should be enough of you,
Barbara, in that woman, she would add:
Child, although you'll not believe this,
there was a time
when they were as real as you;
I seem to recall they lived
then in a small town beside a river
where there were trees and almost every house
had a little plot of grass
around it, sometimes with flowers;
I suppose they drove
to church in the kind of funny old car
you've seen in museums;
and they were young — this was so long ago
that all of the old people were young then;

your great-grandmother
can't have been more than twenty;
the family legend is
she was so lovely, smiling through her tears,
an onlooker compared her to a rainbow.

A Pinch or Two of Dust

— The dust being from Culloden, Scotland,
where, in a battle fought in 1746, the
last of the great Celtic societies was
extinguished.

A friend has given me
a pinch or two of dust,
an ounce at most of soil
from a field where our ancestors,
his and mine, were ploughed into
the compost bed of history, a people
who had outlived their gods,
the last of the old barbarians
destroyed by the first of the new,
magnificent fools who threw
stones and handfuls of earth
at the gunners until they themselves
became part of that earth and thereby
made it theirs for ever,
their blood indistinguishable now
from it, their blood contained
in this pinch or two of dust
as in my body and the body
of the friend who gave it
— this soil not only between
but within
my fingers, a part of
the very cells that shape this poem.

The Rites of Manhood

It's snowing hard enough that the taxis aren't running.
I'm walking home, my night's work finished,
long after midnight, with the whole city to myself,
when across the street I see a very young American sailor
standing over a girl who's kneeling on the sidewalk
and refuses to get up although he's yelling at her
to tell him where she lives so he can take her there
before they both freeze. The pair of them are drunk
and my guess is he picked her up in a bar
and later they got separated from his buddies
and at first it was great fun to play at being
an old salt at liberty in a port full of women with
hinges on their heels, but by now he wants only to
find a solution to the infinitely complex
problem of what to do about her before he falls into
the hands of the police or the shore patrol
— and what keeps this from being squalid is
what's happening to him inside:
if there were other sailors here
it would be possible for him
to abandon her where she is and joke about it
later, but he's alone and the guilt can't be
divided into small forgettable pieces;
he's finding out what it means
to be a man and how different it is
from the way that only hours ago he imagined it.

The Jelly Bean Man

"He carries jelly beans," a neighbour told us
when we first came here. "You're lucky you don't
have any small children."
                           He's the Jelly Bean Man
and the first words he ever said to me
were, "Kiss it and make it well,"
he having observed my wife
bump her forehead against the door
of our car while getting into it
with her arms full of groceries.
"It's nothing to grin about," he said.

So I kissed her above
and between the eyes, and he said,
"Love her; she is the daughter of
Cronos and Rhea, the sister and wife
of Zeus. Here I have a gift for her.
She will share it with you."

And he insisted that she take
two cinnamon rolls
which she and I later ate
at home, very slowly,
with dairy butter
— each bite was like hearing
a little ripple of simple music.

Later we learned it was true
he carried jelly beans and distributed them,
but only as an uncle might or a grandfather
— and, oh, it's so easy to teach
your small daughters and sons
to accept nothing

from strangers, to keep well back always,
to stay out of arm's reach,
to be prepared to run,
so easy to tell them
about evil,
so hard to tell them
about innocence,

so impossible to say:
be good to the Jelly Bean Man
who gives candy to children
from no other motive than love.

The Broadcaster's Poem

I used to broadcast at night
alone in a radio station
but I was never good at it,
partly because my voice wasn't right
but mostly because my peculiar
metaphysical stupidity
made it impossible
for me to keep believing
there was somebody listening
when it seemed I was talking
only to myself in a room no bigger
than an ordinary bathroom.
I could believe it for a while
and then I'd get somewhat
the same feeling as when you
start to suspect you're the victim
of a practical joke.
                    So one part of me
was afraid another part
might blurt out something
about myself so terrible
that even I had never until
that moment suspected it.
                    This was like the fear
of bridges and other
high places: Will I take off my glasses
and throw them
into the water, although I'm
half-blind without them?
Will I sneak up behind
myself and push?
                    Another thing:

as a reporter
I covered an accident in which a train
ran into a car, killing
three young men, one of whom
was beheaded. The bodies looked
boneless, as such bodies do.
More like mounds of rags.
And inside the wreckage
where nobody could get at it
the car radio
was still playing.
                    I thought about places
the disc jockey's voice goes
and the things that happen there
and of how impossible it would be for him
to continue if he really knew.

The Middle-Aged Man in the Supermarket

I'm pretending to test the avocadoes for ripeness
while gaping obliquely at the bare brown legs
of the girl in the orange skirt selecting mushrooms
when she says, "Hi, there, let's make love."
At first I think that she must have caught me
and is being sarcastic and then I decide
she's joking with someone she knows, perhaps the boy
            weighing green beans
or the young man with the watercress, so I try to act
as if I hadn't heard her, walk away at what I hope
is the right speed, without looking back,
and don't stop until I come to
the frozen-food bins, where I'm still standing,
gazing down at things I almost never buy, when
            I become aware
she's near me again, although I see only
a few square inches of brown thigh, a bit of
            orange cloth
and two symmetrical bare feet. I wish I could know
her body so well I could ever afterwards identify her
by taste alone. I rattle a carton
of frozen peas, read both French and English
            directions
on a package of frozen bread dough. She still
            stands there.
I wait for her to say to me:
"I fell in love the moment I saw you.
I want us to spend our first week together
in bed. We'll have our meals sent up. I'm even
            prettier
when I'm bare and I promise I'll keep my eyes shut
while you're naked, so that you'll never worry
that I might be comparing your body with that

of a previous lover, none of whom was older
than twenty, although the truth is I like
fat hips and big bellies — it's a kink
        that I have:
my nipples harden when I envision
those mountainous moons of flesh above me."

Full Circle

In my youth, no one spoke of love
where I lived, except I spoke of it,
and then only in the dark. The word was known
like the name of a city on another continent.
No one called anyone his friend,
although they had friends. Perhaps they were afraid
to commit so much of themselves,
to demand so much of others; for if they'd said,
"We're friends," as they never did,
it would have been a contract.
As it was, they could quarrel,
even hit one another if they were drunk,
and remain friends, never having said it.
Where nothing was sworn there could be no betrayal.
Nor did they touch
casually; their persons seemed to occupy
more space than their bodies did.
Seeing an adult run we'd have looked first for the reason
in the direction from which he came. We never met trains;
my people were like that.
                              It was not enough for me.
"I love you," I said.
Whispered it, painfully, and was laughed at;
hid until the wounds healed and said it again,
            muttered it.
Wanting to be loved, "I love you," was what I said.
And I learned to touch, as a legless man
learns to walk again.
                              Came to live among people
who called anyone a friend
who was not an enemy, to whom there were no strangers:
because there were so many, they were invisible.
Now, like everyone else, I send

postcards to acquaintances, With Love —
Love meaning, I suppose, that I remember the recipients
kindly and wish them well. But I say it
less often and will not be surprised
at myself if the time comes when I do not say it,
when I do not touch, except desperately, when I ask
nothing more of others, but greet them with a wink,
as my grandfather might have done, looking up
for an instant from his carpenter's bench.

The Visitor

Last summer we found a sleeping bag
in our back yard, under the cedars
where we don't mow the grass.
Someone had slept there.

A friend had arrived late
the previous night, we decided,
and hadn't wanted to wake us.
He'd got up early and gone
to see someone else.

We stayed home all day and waited for him.

But nobody came. And the sleeping bag
was still there next morning
although it hadn't been slept in:
you can tell a bed that's been used
recently from one that hasn't
been — the disorder of
the former is in sharper focus.

Should we have brought it inside?
Should we have called the police
on the second day or the third
or the fourth? Perhaps. As it was
we forgot about it

until this spring
when we crammed it into a garbage can.
I think it was its rottenness, the sick
feel of it in my hands
that made me believe something
horrible could have happened

to whoever it was
that lay down that night
on the ground within fifty feet
of our house, just outside the light
from the bulb above the back door

or, if nothing harmed him,
that he ran away,
that young man with terrible eyes,
because he wasn't sure he could resist
temptation a second night:
for he must have watched us,
moving about the kitchen,
sitting down to dinner,
getting ready for bed,

he could have attacked us while we slept,
and how can we be sure he won't come back?

On the Barrens

"Once when we were hunting cattle
               on the barrens,"
so began many of the stories they told,
gathered in the kitchen, a fire still
               the focus of life then,
the teapot on the stove as long as
               anyone was awake,
mittens and socks left to thaw on
               the open oven door,
chunks of pine and birch piled
               halfway to the ceiling,
and always a faint smell of smoke
               like spice in the air,
the lamps making their peace with
               the darkness,
the world not entirely answerable
               to man.

They took turns talking, the listeners
               puffed their pipes,
he whose turn it was to speak used his
               as an instrument,
took his leather pouch from a pocket
               of his overalls,
gracefully, rubbed tobacco between
               his rough palms
as he set the mood, tamped it into
               the bowl
at a moment carefully chosen, scratched
               a match when it was necessary
to prolong the suspense. If his pipe
               went out it was no accident,

if he spat in the stove it was done
          for a purpose.
When he finished he might lean back
          in his chair so that it stood
on two legs; there'd be a short silence.

The barrens were flat clay fields,
          twenty miles from the sea
and separated from it by dense woods
          and farmlands.
They smelled of salt and the wind
          blew there
constantly as it does on the shore
          of the North Atlantic.

There had been a time, the older men
          said, when someone had owned
the barrens but something had happened
long ago and now anyone who wanted to
          could pasture there.
The cattle ran wild all summer,
sinewy little beasts, ginger-coloured
          with off-white patches,
grazed there on the windswept barrens
          and never saw a human
until fall when the men came to round
          them up,
sinewy men in rubber boots and tweed caps
          with their dogs beside them.

Some of the cattle would by now have
          forgotten
there'd been a time before they'd
          lived on the barrens.
They'd be truly wild, dangerous, the
          men would loose the dogs on them,

mongrel collies, barn dogs with the
        dispositions of convicts
who are set over their fellows,
        the dogs would go for the nose,
sink their teeth in the tender flesh,
        toss the cow on its side,
bleating, hooves flying, but shortly
        tractable.
There were a few escaped,
        it was said, and in a little while
they were like no other cattle —
        the dogs feared them,
they roared at night and the men
        lying by their camp-fires
heard them and moaned in their sleep,
        the next day tracking them
found where they'd pawed the moss,
        where their horns had scraped
bark from the trees — all the stories
        agreed
in this: now there was nothing to do
        but kill them.

Land and Sea

Old men repeat themselves.
In other words: speak songs.

Can't let the sea be,
the land can't.
                    Won't ever
leave her in peace.
                    Has to keep
troubling the waters,
the land does.
                    This from
Captain Thorburn Greenough
of Hall's Harbour who, in his prime,
could have sailed a bucket
through hell with his handkerchief,
they say.

The land won't let the sea be.

You'd of sailed under
canvas, you'd of knowed that.
Wouldn't of needed me
to tell you.
                    The shore!
We never felt safe
till we was out of her reach.

The Red Wool Shirt

I was hanging out my wash,
says the woman in North Sydney.
It was a rope line I was using
and they were wooden pins,
the real old-fashioned kind
that didn't have a spring.

It was good drying weather.

I could see the weir fishermen
at work.
          I had a red wool shirt
in my hands and had just
noticed that one of the buttons
was missing.

Then I looked up and saw
Charlie Sullivan coming
towards me.
He'd always had a funny walk.
It was as if he was walking
sideways.
          That walk of his
always made me smile except
for some reason
I didn't smile
that day.
          He had on a hat
with salmon flies
that he'd tied himself
in the brim.

Poor old Charlie.

It's bad, Mary, he said.

I finished
hanging up the red wool
shirt
        and then I said,
Charlie, it's not
both of them, and he said,
Mary, I'm afraid it is.

And that was that.

What Colour Is Manitoba?

My son, in Grade III or IV
and assigned to make a map,
asked us, what colour is
Manitoba? and refused to believe
it didn't matter, provided
it wasn't the same
as Saskatchewan and Ontario.
I remember his face.
I've seldom observed
such constrained rage
except in small children
and university professors.

But it's a common failing,
this excessive faith
in one method of denoting
boundaries. In his atlas
at school, Manitoba was
purple-brown. Similarly,
the road maps indicate
that I live less than
five hundred miles
from my birthplace.

There are truer charts.

I'd never once used
a telephone
in the nineteen years
before I left there,
had never eaten a hamburger;
I could milk a cow by hand
or yoke an ox, knew a man who

once as a passenger
in a heavily-loaded
stage coach inching up
one side of a very steep
hill in California
had got off to walk
and as a result of this
— the downward slope
being equally precipitous,
the horses being compelled
by the weight behind them
to gallop and he having to
run to catch up —
was mistaken by the driver
for a highwayman, and shot:
the scar was still there
after fifty years.
Little else had changed
in our village since
the mid-eighteenth century
when Coulon de Villiers
passed through with his troops,
seven years before
he defeated young George
Washington at Fort Necessity.
Scraps of grape-shot worked
their way to the surface
of the earth the way bits
of shrapnel are said to
emerge at last through the skin
of an old soldier.

Add to all this
that it wasn't the same
for everybody, even there.

My family was poor.
Not disadvantaged — curse
that word of the sniffling
middle classes, suggesting
as it does that there's
nothing worse than
not being like them.
We were poor — curse that word, too,
as a stroke victim
half-maddened by his inability
to utter a certain phrase
will say "shit" instead
and be understood.

A sociologist,
belonging by definition to
one of the lesser
of the ruling sub-castes,
comes from Columbia University
to study a community
in Nova Scotia not very different
from where I was born.
A Tutsi witch doctor among Hutus.
He finds, according to
the New York Times, that
almost everyone he meets is crazy.

It's as if a chemist
had analyzed a river
and declared that its water
was an inferior form of fire.

There are secrets I share
with the very old. I know why
we fought in the Boer War

and how in the lumber camps
we cracked the lice between
our thumbnails and it made
a homely sound, was a restful
occupation of an evening:
cracking lice, we were
like women knitting.

Altogether apart
from that, I bear tribal
marks, ritual mutilations.
My brothers and sisters
fill the slums of every
city in North America.
(God knows this is no boast.)
The poor, whom the Russians
used to call the Dark People,
as if it were in the blood.
I know their footsteps.
We meet each other's eyes.

It's Good to Be Here

I'm in trouble, she said
to him. That was the first
time in history that anyone
had ever spoken of me.

It was 1932 when she
was just fourteen years old
and men like him
worked all day for
one stinking dollar.

There's quinine, she said.
That's bullshit, he told her.

Then she cried and then
for a long time neither of them
said anything at all and then
their voices kept rising until
they were screaming at each other
and then there was another long silence and then
they began to talk very quietly and at last he said,
well, I guess we'll just have to make the best of it.

While I lay curled up,
my heart beating,
in the darkness inside her.

My Beard, Once Lionheart Red

My beard, once Lionheart red, is now yellowish-gray
like a rainy sunset; a child, having seen the statue
in the Victoria and Albert Museum, of Silenus, the satyr
and foster father of Bacchus, and then noticing me
in the crowd, embarrassed her parents by pointing out
the resemblance; and yet, strange to say, I am happier
than when I was a boy and might have passed for the
    messenger
from Apollo to Helen, had I worn my hair long, and been
    naked, and had I known.

Happier, I suppose because I have all but abandoned
    hope of ever reaching
the lost island of answers, of ever catching up
    with the tribe
that left me behind as a baby, of meeting my real parents,
the King and Queen, of being adopted officially by God.

Happier, I suppose because I expect less and less
of everybody; where once I wanted all of creation to
    love me,
I am now almost content to have my presence acknowledged
with a semblance of kindness and a measure of grace.
I rarely make a nuisance of myself, as I so often used to do,
by passing out love, left and right, as if giving away
    kittens.

Happier, I suppose because I have tasted enough of fame
to know that it is not flavoured with sugar, as I
    had thought
when I studied it hungrily in pictures, but with salt;
and, also, that the potion does not transform the one
    who drinks it,

but instead creates for him an illusionary twin, in
     whose activities
his part, whether of proud or bemused brother,
is never more than peripheral; people seem to sense this,
for they treat him as if he were not altogether real,
will say to him, casually and with no apparent wish to
     be other than polite,
how amazing it is to find him so fat when he is known
     to be dying, slowly, of cancer.

Happier, I suppose because I was bound hand and foot,
     sewn in a blanket, thrown
into the pool of the man-eating crab, and broke free,
bearing wounds that will tug at me always, like the claws
of beggars, so that I cannot forget how wonderful it is
to get out of bed, stand up and walk, pick up a glass,
fill it with water, lift it to my mouth, and drink, with
     only enough pain
involved in each phase of the process to remind me that
     I am fortune's child, and richly blessed.

What Happened When He Went to the Store for Bread

for Michael Brian Oliver

Because I went to the store for bread
one afternoon when I was eighteen
and arrived there just in time to meet
and be introduced to a man who had stopped
for a bottle of Coca-Cola (I've forgotten his name),
and because this man invited me to visit
a place where I met another man who gave me
the address of yet another man,
this one in another province,
and because I wrote a letter and got an answer
which took me away from the place where I was born,
I am who I am instead of being somebody else.

What would I have been if I hadn't left there
when I did? I would have almost certainly
gone mad; I think I might have killed somebody.
But even if something else had saved me
from madness, I would not be the same person.
I'd have spent thirty years in a different world
and come to look at things in such a different way
that even my memories of childhood and youth
would be different; it might even seem to me now
that there was never anything to escape from.

And then too, there are those who are other
than they would have been, because of some small act
of mine; I played a certain record once
because I liked it, and because he liked it too,
    a stranger
became my friend and, as such, met the woman

he married, and now they have two children
who would not have been born except for my taste
    in music.

Carrying the thought farther still, there must be
people in cities that I've never visited
whose lives have changed, perhaps not because of what
I've written but because I wrote: it might be
they didn't like my play and so left early
and because they left early something happened
that would not have happened if they'd stayed —
I put it that way so as not to sound immodest.
God knows, there's not a lot to boast about
when so much seems to depend upon the time of day
a boy goes out to buy a loaf of bread.

A Pair of Pruning Shears

The trees around this house are killing one
another. This summer, the maple and the fir
sucked the life from the spruce, having first
shut it off from the rain and then walled in its roots
with theirs, so that at last it died in a desert
five feet in diameter. The maple still
bears wounds from that struggle, a withered limb
for instance, and now the fir has turned against
its old ally and bars it from the sun,
while, a little distance away, the young birches
gnaw away at the beech and will bring her down
unless she succeeds in smothering them first;
and, afterwards, the winners will go at it —
"You ought to have pruned them," a neighbour says,
who knows about such matters. "It's the same
with everything," he tells me. "Even rhubarb.
Look at that fine patch you inherited from
the former tenants, gone to weed because
you didn't take a knife to it. It needed
to be cut back almost to the roots last season.
Now it's too late." So I start with the rose-bushes
that were so elegant when we moved here but now
have sprouted hideous tentacles, each of them
black and bare except for a few red flowers
at the tip where, if this were a different kind
of horror story, there would be a mouth.
I take a knife, a saw, a pair of shears,
waiting until it's almost dark because,
being awkward at such tasks, I'd rather not
be watched, and drinking a quick double gin
because I'm loath to destroy anything,
never knowing where it might lead or end;
I take a knife, a saw, a pair of shears,

and soon I'm breathing hard and there is sweat
in my eyes and my heart is saying no, no, no,
reminding me that this body of mine is
a rickety Empire, in no shape for war,
Byzantium in 1450, Turkey
in 1914; I saw off the tentacles,
and scissor at the live, green undergrowth,
the thorns making me think of Gulliver
and the Lilliputian archers; there is blood
on my hands and forearms when I stop; the walk
is buried in debris, with a few spots
of red on the black and green: they're the flowers
that ought to have been mouths; because of them,
it is as if the bushes had bled too.

I'm still sitting there when the stars appear,
another drink beside me on the steps,
my rested heart now saying yes, no, yes,
but in a little while I'll go inside
to wait for spring. How good it would be then
to come out and look down at the black stumps
of the rose-bushes, stumps like rotten molars,
and see there in the grass a different shade
of green, one touched with gold, new growth,
the fresh stalks as supple as the partner in
a boy's lascivious dream, and glorious,
glorious and absurd, in the way of all
such living things that reach up to the sun
to touch it, though they've risen only scant
inches above the earth — an argument,
perhaps, although admittedly a weak one,
against the rumours, widespread and persuasive,
of Death's total, unconditional victory.

The Seasick Sailor, and Others

The awkward young sailor who is always seasick
is the one who will write about ships.
The young man whose soldiering consists in the
     delivery
of candy and cigarettes to the front
is the one who will write about war.
The man who will never learn to drive a car
and keeps going home to his mother
is the one who will write about the road.

Stranger still, hardly anyone else will write
     so well
about the sea or war or the road. And then there
     is the woman
who has scarcely spoken to a man except her
     brother
and who works in a room no larger than a
     closet,
she will write as well as anyone who ever
     lived
about vast, open spaces and the desires of
     the flesh;
and that other woman who will live with her
     sister
and rarely leave her village, she will excel
in portraying men and women in society;
and that woman, in some ways the most wonderful
     of them all,
who is afraid to go outdoors, who hides when
     someone knocks,
she will write great poems about the universe
     inside her.

A Night in 1938, and the Night After

The first time I saw electric
light, the Queen of Heaven
appeared. This was not light
to see by, this was
light to marvel at. All
evening we sat, adults
as well as children, in that
light and did nothing
else. Next day we waited
for Uncle, as head of the
family, to decide the time
had come to switch it on
again. I held my breath
as he pulled the chain, but
the Queen of Heaven did not
return. In a little while,
the adults picked up
the playing cards. Oh!
how I despised them
for that. Then I saw
that the shadows were
gone, the places where
I could roll myself into
a ball or kneel or stand very
still, and not be seen.
I used to do that
and listen. Sometimes, I would
slip out of the shadows when
nobody was looking and
switch cards on them. It was hard
to keep from laughing then.
Now, no matter how
small, quick or quiet

I was, I would never
again have that power.
I could never again
make myself invisible.

Why are you crying?
Uncle asked me.

There Is a Horrible Wing to the Hotel

There is a horrible wing to the hotel.
Unspeakable things happen there.

The toilets are plugged.
There is excrement on the floors
and urine in the bathtubs.

In one room I saw a dog
eating a kitten.

And people live there.
Like that young man with muscular arms
who mistook me for a thief
and would have beaten me with a club
except that I refused to fight back,
knowing that he was so much stronger
that it would be no use.

We became friends, he and I,
and there was a boy who stole
two small triangular pieces
of copper or bronze
from the young man's room
and gave them to me —
I think they may once have been
attached to a trophy.

I hid them when the young man came looking
for them, because I was afraid
of being beaten, and watched him beat the boy.

But one night on the roof we released balloons
in the shape of little animals;
there was a bear, for instance, and a giraffe
which was bright red, and a blue rhinoceros.

They flew very high, those balloons,
and I am afraid of heights, yet I watched them
like everybody else, until they vanished
into that enormous, spinning funnel of blackness.

They flew very high and fast,
and I have never seen anything that looked so free.

He Visits the Shrine of a Saint

Whenever I see the indentations left in granite
by the knees of generation after generation
of human beings, not all of them worshippers,
some of them, doubtless, only carrying out
what was then a social obligation, others not very
different from the poker player who gets up
when his luck is bad and, by way of incantation,
walks once around the table, still others whose
    purpose
was to please somebody, perhaps a parent out of
    kindness,
perhaps a superior out of fear or ambition
in an age when Mother Church could make an Emperor
or cause a King to submit to the lash,
whenever I look at such marks in a slab of stone
and reflect that most of those who helped to make them
have left no further trace of their passage,
it hardly matters to me whether faith or folly
moved them (when addressing mysteries for which
there are no words in any language, it seems only sensible
to give proper names to the more benign ones,
such as hope fulfilled, and to call them saints);
what does matter is that they came here, to this
    place,
and here performed a supremely human gesture;
I'm reminded of how Xerxes felt when he looked out
    at that vast army,
and it came to him that not one of them would be
    alive
in another hundred years; that was 2,500 years ago,
and he wept; but this is not so sad as that: when I
    envisage
all of those ardent pilgrims in the dust

and think of how they each made their minute imprint
and then vanished, thousands upon thousands
of them, none much wiser, none a bigger fool
than I have been, none guilty of a crime
I could not have committed, none much better
(not even the saint himself) than I might have been,
then I am almost at peace with the knowledge
of how quickly time will close the little space
        between us,
and my breath become one with theirs and the wind;
and so, laughing at myself as at any other
child doing something quaint, I say a prayer,
and might kneel down, if I could do it
without feeling fraudulent or being seen,
and if I could be certain that I had the right.

The Secretive Fishermen

It is dusk now, and the secretive fishermen
are trolling for boys on the highways
north and south of here: a tradition.
It is what you do when you work in a bank,
for instance, or for the government,
and share your neighbor's hunger but not his tastes.
You drive back and forth, back and forth,
in the twilight, and it can be dangerous;
men have been killed for it, and not one
of their murderers has ever been convicted.
Yet they are peaceable men, even timorous
about most things, men of moderate views
and modest ambitions, whose daytime dress
is always quietly correct; for the most part,
they have always lived here, and their fathers
worked for the bank or the government before them.
If they were married, it would be to women
much like their mothers, who belonged to
the usual organizations, cooked the usual meals,
and thought the usual thoughts. Instead,
out of necessity, the meek and mild accountant
rides out in search of adventure like
the Red Shadow, and Sir Percy Blakeney
risks death as the Scarlet Pimpernel,
except that this time the road is real,
just as the boys are not made of glossy paper
and therefore cannot be undressed
with a flick of the fingers turning over a page
nor be made to disappear in the same way:
they are co-authors and may change the script,
out of fear or disgust or because it amuses them,
so that it ends badly, with the Pimpernel
beaten bloody, the Red Shadow turned into

a monstrous parody of a baby-fat two-year-old,
blubbering, and naked except for an undershirt.
Still, it rarely comes to that; there must even be times
when it is almost perfect, in its way: two strangers,
each of them a tourist exploring the Mexico
that is the other's body. It can't always be
as sad as dusk for those lonesome travellers.

Legacy
— adapted from the Romanian of Tudor Arghezi

All that I'll leave you when I die is a name
    in a book
which they'll say is mine. Take it in the
    long evening
which stretches all the way from my farthest
    ancestors to you,
across the ravines and ditches which they
    bridged or climbed,
and you too, so young, are expected to conquer.
The book is only a single step, yet it is your
    solemn charter,
won by slaves and serfs who strained beneath
    their loads:
sacks filled with their own bones, handed down
    to me.

So that I could change a spade into a pen,
our ancestors suffered together with their oxen,
and gathered the sweat of a hundred years to
    give me ink.
I kneaded the words that they spoke to their cattle
until they were transformed into visions and icons.
Out of their rags, I made wreaths; and from old
    poisons
I made honey. From their hearths I took
the ashes of the dead and made them live again
in a god of stone and paper who holds the world
in his lap and watches over you.
All the pain and sorrow of our people

I put into a single violin
and as the master heard it played
he danced like a he-goat in the spring.
We withstood the whip, and now the lash turns into
    words
and becomes a live growth that spreads in the air,
bearing at its tip, like a grape, the fruit
of ancient and endless sorrow.

However soft her bed may be when she reads it,
the Princess will suffer in my book;
for words of fire and steel are mingled with
    the soft whisper
in the book that a slave wrote and the lord
    reads without knowing
that in its depths there lies all the rage
    of my forefathers.

I'm Simply Walking

I'm simply walking,
I think.
Or standing there.
I'm not afraid,
which means the
homicidal maniac
must be dead.

I can't tell where I am,
but that is only because
there has been no reason
for me to ask myself:
what place is this?

Nothing horrible
has happened.

I'm simply walking,
except
this time I'm not a man;
I'm a woman.

The most extraordinary
thing about this
is that it is
of no importance.

Perhaps that's because
there's nobody else here.

I put one foot in front
of the other
and think no more
about being a woman
than a woman would.

If I'm wearing a dress,
well, what of it,
I must be accustomed to
wearing dresses.

It's nothing at all like
putting on your sister's
panties and frock
when you were twelve
and wanting to be seen
like that,
but please God never
recognized.

Watch me, Sir
Looking Glass!
You said then,
and twirled
like a top

until you thought
how awful it must be
to bleed like that.

He Reflects Upon His Own Stupidity
for Michael Pacey

For the first twenty-five years of my life
I never met anyone who was stupid
in quite the same way as I am.

Oh, I knew many, many people
who would have been judged subnormal
by a professional psychologist
— for whatever that is worth:
not much, I imagine, since almost all
the professional psychologists I've run into
have been lunatics or fools.

But I never met anyone who was an idiot
about doors, as I am. I turn my hotel key
this way and that, that way and this,
can seldom get out of a car without help.

If we were measured by our success with locks,
I would be assessed as possibly trainable,
but certainly not educable.

I'm equally stupid about many other things.
And, dear God, it used to be lonely.

But now almost everyone I know is stupid
in much the same way as I am.
Not merely my friends but casual acquaintances,
yes, and enemies too, keep locking themselves out,
and getting lost,
and have trouble changing a tire.

My stupidity matches theirs.
I have found my tribe and am more at home in the world.

Great Things Have Happened

We were talking about the great things
that have happened in our lifetimes;
and I said, "Oh, I suppose the moon landing
was the greatest thing that has happened
in my time." But, of course, we were all lying.
The truth is the moon landing didn't mean
one-tenth as much to me as one night in 1963
when we lived in a three-room flat in what once
    had been
the mansion of some Victorian merchant prince
(our kitchen had been a clothes closet, I'm sure),
on a street where by now nobody lived
who could afford to live anywhere else.
That night, the three of us, Claudine, Johnnie and me,
woke up at half-past four in the morning
and ate cinnamon toast together.

"Is that all?" I hear somebody ask.

Oh, but we were silly with sleepiness
and, under our windows, the street-cleaners
were working their machines and conversing in
    Italian, and
everything was strange without being threatening,
even the tea-kettle whistled differently
than in the daytime: it was like the feeling
you get sometimes in a country you've never visited
before, when the bread doesn't taste quite the same,
the butter is a small adventure, and they put
paprika on the table instead of pepper,
except that there was nobody in this country
except the three of us, half-tipsy with the wonder
of being alive, and wholly enveloped in love.

How Beautiful Art Thy Feet with Shoes

I suppose it's because so many
poets and artists have never had enough
love from women — as boys they were hideous
in their own eyes, as I was, who thought myself
half-brother to Quasimodo
and looked upon every girl as Esmeralda —
I suppose it's because of this
that they've devoted so much time
to portraying the wonders
of her nakedness, to celebrating
her thighs and breasts
so that some love poems sound more like
commercials for fried chicken,
and hardly ever mention
moments like this when I look up and see you,
through the window, getting out of a cab
with your arms full of Christmas parcels
(they always seem to be
Christmas parcels, even in July and even if
they're only books from the public library)
there must have been times, many times,
over the years, when you came home from somewhere
without your arms filled with parcels,
but I don't remember any of them now,
nor do I recall a time when you didn't come in
either bursting to show me something
or trying to hide something from me:
I've never known anybody so fond of arranging
surprises or so inept at keeping secrets;
and I know how long it takes you to complete
the smallest transaction, how much you like to
look at things and touch them, and how you're always
getting involved in long conversations with

old men in waiting rooms, little kids on tricycles,
the high school students who work part-time in supermarkets,
how you even say, "Hello, dog," if you meet one —
all this, and so much more, goes through my head
as I catch a glimpse of you, getting out of a cab
with your arms full of parcels, as they always are,
and am reminded, suddenly, of how much I love you.

The Thief

Having myself been scared silly when I was young
of any girl made of flesh and, God help us, blood,
I am in sympathy with the boy, said to be slow but
   not retarded,
who has been taken into custody for stealing panties
from the laundry rooms in our apartment building.
They say he had a trunkful of them. It reminds me
of those other thieves, treated as praiseworthy,
in the old folk tales; Jack of Jack and the Beanstalk
climbing in through a window of a castle to snitch a
   harp;
it was no crime to rob a giant in those days.
If the King heard about it, he gave the thief his
   daughter
in marriage; and, as everybody knows that carried
   with it a guarantee
of living happily ever after. Mind you, that was
   well before
the invention of panties; for that matter, drawers
   of any kind
are believed to have been unknown before the 16th
   century
and, naturally, are first mentioned in a sermon
by the Cardinal-Archbishop of Milan in which he said
   that God Almighty
intended woman to keep her bottom bare, in
   remembrance
of Mother Eve's weakness. All that was long, long
   ago,
and once upon a time; but I can tell you this from
   experience:
that to a boy like that — who would even today trade
   his cow, if he had one,

for a handful of beans, not so much because he was
    a fool
as because he was too bashful to argue, and
    afterwards
hate himself with an almost murderous hatred for being
    such a bumpkin —
to a boy like that, every female, without exception,
is a giantess, ready and able to grind his bones to
    bake her bread.

Bobby Sands

for Robert Weaver

I did not cry for Bobby Sands, but I almost did,
thinking of my grandmother whom I loved, and who
    loved me,
and of how her voice would break when she told me again
how her grandmother died in a field in County Wexford
with green stains on her lips, her hands filled with
    grass,
and of how in that same year the English wagons
escorted by English troops carried Irish grain
down to English vessels for shipment to England.
    Yes,
yes, that was a long, long time ago; but somebody
    should
remember Mary Foley, somebody should weep for her,
even if it is only a drunken listener
to lying ballads. Being human, we
each of us can bear no more than a particle
of pain that is not our own; the rest is rhetoric.
Better to shed a tear for Mary Foley
than to rant or babble about suffering
that is beyond our capacity to comprehend.
And what of Bobby Sands? We talk too much,
all of us. In common decency, don't speak
of him unless you have gone at least a day
without food, and be sure you understand
that he loved being alive, the same as you.
Then say what you like. Call him a fool.
Call him a criminal. You'll get no argument
from me. I'll agree with everything
you say in dispraise of gunmen. Oh, but Mary Foley's
ghost was left in my keeping.
I know in my heart that if he had come to me
for a place to hide I could never have shut him out.

He Sits Down on the Floor of a School for the Retarded

I sit down on the floor of a school for the retarded,
a writer of magazine articles accompanying a band
that was met at the door by a child in a man's body
who asked them, "Are you the surprise they promised us?"

It's Ryan's Fancy, Dermot on guitar,
Fergus on banjo, Denis on penny-whistle.
In the eyes of this audience, they're everybody
who has ever appeared on TV. I've been telling lies
to a boy who cried because his favourite detective
hadn't come with us; I said he had sent his love
and, no, I didn't think he'd mind if I signed his name
to a scrap of paper: when the boy took it, he said,
"Nobody will ever get this away from me,"
in the voice, more hopeless than defiant,
of one accustomed to finding that his hiding places
have been discovered, used to having objects snatched
out of his hands. Weeks from now I'll send him
another autograph, this one genuine
in the sense of having been signed by somebody
on the same payroll as the star.
Then I'll feel less ashamed. Now everyone is singing,
"Old MacDonald had a farm," and I don't know what to do

about the young woman (I call her a woman
because she's twenty-five at least, but think of her
as a little girl, she plays that part so well,
having known no other), about the young woman who
sits down beside me and, as if it were the most natural
thing in the world, rests her head on my shoulder.

It's nine o'clock in the morning, not an hour for music.
And, at the best of times, I'm uncomfortable

in situations where I'm ignorant
of the accepted etiquette: it's one thing
to jump a fence, quite another thing to blunder
into one in the dark. I look around me
for a teacher to whom to smile out my distress.
They're all busy elsewhere. "Hold me," she whispers. "Hold me."

I put my arm around her. "Hold me tighter."
I do, and she snuggles closer. I half-expect
someone in authority to grab her
or me; I can imagine this being remembered
for ever as the time the sex-crazed writer
publicly fondled the poor retarded girl.
"Hold me," she says again. What does it matter
what anybody thinks? I put my other arm around her,
rest my chin in her hair, thinking of children
real children, and of how they say it, "Hold me,"
and of a patient in a geriatric ward
I once heard crying out to his mother, dead
for half a century, "I'm frightened! Hold me!"
and of a boy-soldier screaming it on the beach
at Dieppe, of Nelson in Hardy's arms,
of Frieda gripping Lawrence's ankle
until he sailed off in his Ship of Death.

It's what we all want, in the end,
to be held, merely to be held,
to be kissed (not necessarily with the lips,
for every touching is a kind of kiss).

Yes, it's what we all want, in the end,
not to be worshipped, not to be admired,
not to be famous, not to be feared,
not even to be loved, but simply to be held.

She hugs me now, this retarded woman, and I hug her.
We are brother and sister, father and daughter,
mother and son, husband and wife.
We are lovers. We are two human beings
huddled together for a little while by the fire
in the Ice Age, two hundred thousand years ago.

A Song to Be Whispered

Your body consists of so many provinces
that I, a man of salt, must break off my fingers
one by one —
                    like so!

See how they fly,
become birds in an orchard.

Oh, my love, it was
God Himself who wove
the skin that clothes you.

Yet the eunuch who escorts
Bathsheba to the King's House
mutters, as always,
"No good can come of it."

You Can't Get There from Here

There is almost always a lilac bush — lilac was the smell
of my childhood, a fine free smell that sets colts galloping
along cool rivers in my mind — and there are almost always
red rose bushes and, sometimes, an apple tree
or even an orchard, where the deer feed on windfalls; and in
    the tall grass
you may come upon a pair of sheep shears, like monstrous
    scissors but made in one piece
as tweezers are, and a grub-hoe, like a two-bitted axe
except that one bit is a hammer; and if you dare to go inside
what remains of the house, there could be a schooner
on the floor at the head of the stairs to the cellar,
its three-foot-long hull on its side, its masts broken, its rigging
rotted; and we'll be there watching
from the dark by the vegetable bins — there was never any
light to switch on, and you'll not have brought with you
a lantern to find us,
but we will see you; oh, we will see you.

Two Visitors from Utah

for Nancy Bauer

The doorbell rings.
        I come face to face with myself.
Myself of 1955, when I was more than a quarter of a century
younger. Two boys with the kind of haircuts
that seem designed to instill humility.
                Their suits and ties
make them move as young soldiers do
when on leave, almost demurely.
          Of course they're Mormons
who go as missionaries somewhat
as young English aristocrats used to go
on the Grand Tour,
              except that their purpose
is not to learn but to teach.
         Shall I tell them I love
their Prophet and that, like him,
             I was a farmboy
who opened the Bible like a door
and saw no difference
between the hill where he went for the cows
       and the hill where the King-to-be,
              young David, tended his sheep?

Oh, we knew,
       Joseph Smith and I,
             that it had all happened
a long, long time ago like the stories our grandparents
told us about their grandparents.
           But we had touched the stone
on which Abraham would have sacrificed
his son, if God had been less merciful;
        and if word had come —
a neighbour shouting it —

that there were Philistines encamped
                        by the river in which we swam,
            and a giant leading them,
we would not have been surprised.
We would have fetched our sling-shots.

                    Shall I tell them
            that I too went barefoot
            all summer (the worst of it was running
            on fresh-cut hayfields, the stubble like toothpicks;
            Joe Smith would have known that);
and, still barefoot, talked with an angel of the Lord
            who spoke in Jacobean English?
                    Shall I tell them
that I know their Prophet better than they ever could?
            I love him because he wrestled
            with the farmboys who followed him
            out of Egypt —
                        try to picture Moses,
Confucius, Buddha, Zoroaster, Mohammad or Jesus
            wrestling,
                        rolling over and over on the ground
            not in holy frenzy,
            but for the sheer fun of it.
                        He said that being
a Prophet was a part-time thing
            (just as a poet is a poet only
            while writing a poem).
                        He also danced —
not with the Holy Spirit, but with women,
whom he desired so much that he could never
have called down the wrath of the Lord upon Bathsheba
as Nathan did.
                        He taught that even God
            had a body like ours,

and that we could become
gods — which would suggest
that our God was once every bit as human
as we are,
that before he created our universe
he too danced and wrestled and made love,
even cursed and swore as the Prophet Joseph did
when he was not being a Prophet.

1914–1918

Thinking again of all those young men who were given
    the same first name,
Canada, once they had reached the place which we in our
    innocence then
called *Overseas*, doubtless with the same intonation
as Frankish peasants had used eight centuries earlier
in speaking of the sons who had followed their steely Lords
    to *Outre Mar*;
thinking of how a German officer remembered this for half
    a century as the strangest thing
he saw in four years of war — the Canadians walking,
simply walking, in no apparent order, but like any group
    of men going anywhere,
into a hailstorm of machine-gun fire that flattened
    them like wheat,
"They did not even look like soldiers, yet fought like
    Prussian Guards,"
I wish, as they would have done, who were much like me,
though they were so much younger, that God's bad brother,
having killed them, had said *Enough!* and had not
    proceeded
to prove their deaths were pointless; if they had to
    die
(and all of us do; oh, all of us do), then I wish
that we could say that we are who we are because they
    were who they were.
That much, at least, has been given others. I think of
    names:
Salamanca, Antietam, Leningrad. I think of Polish
    miners
singing of Polish horsemen, a Cuban schoolchild placing
    flowers
at a wall filled with old photographs.

                    All of it lies,
perhaps, or romantic rubbish, though those young men
        would not have thought it was.

My country has no history, only a past.

Driving a Hard Bargain

What would cause a man to haggle over the price
of the rifle which, later that same day,
he used to kill himself?
                              As a young reporter,
I thought, "Capitalism!"
                              The poor bastard knew what it was
to ask the landlord if he'd wait another week, and then
thank him for answering, "I don't seem to have much choice
in the matter, do I?" in the tone of voice
and with the facial expression of a gentleman
on horseback tapping his boot with a whip,
knew what it was like to make his wife cry every payday
as men on low wages almost always do (it begins with an
     argument
over some small luxury — perhaps a gift one has bought for
     the other, a bottle of wine
to celebrate her birthday, a colour TV she has secretly rented
for him to watch the Grey Cup game — and the realization
that because of it something else will now have to be
endured or postponed or done without or given up.)
"No," the sales clerk said. "This guy was loaded."
"Drunk?" "Nah, loaded with dough. And guess how much
he made me knock off the price. Are you ready for this?
Two measly bucks."
                              Could it have been habit then?
I once knew the owner of a substantial business
who, after his secretary had gone home, searched through
     the wastebaskets
for envelopes that bore uncancelled postage stamps.
The same man had gone in at night or on a weekend
and, with a screwdriver, adjusted the softdrink machines,
so that they'd not disgorge the bottle-caps,
some of which were worth two dollars in a contest.

He might have dickered in the face of death.
I don't know. I do know that for twenty years
I've wondered about that man who killed himself.
Perhaps, when in the store, he was not yet aware
of how he would use the rifle. Perhaps he expected
to go on a hunting trip with friends. Enough can happen
in an hour to make a man decide he'd rather
be dead.
          Or, for whatever reason, would he still be
alive if the clerk had refused to sell for any less?

Home from the Wars
for Walter Learning

His hand in his mother's, her
scented with dried rose petals
and spearmint, the whole city
turned upside down, spilling out a torrent
of people, the flood rushing down
to the harbour where even the cloth flags
joined in the clapping and the ships' horns
wallowed in it —

"There's your father!" she said.
But there were so many,
all the same greenish-brown
scum and mud colour,
so many of them on the decks
of the troopship, looking down
as if from a cloud in a nightmare,
every last one of them
judging him,
it seemed, and his mother
had let go.

But he didn't cry
until he hung suspended
in the air while the stranger's
coarse wool sandpapered his face;
and he's not sure if it was then
or in memory years afterwards that he saw
a gull die in each of the man's eyes
as they do when small boys with fishing lines
hook them
and he cried again.

He Attempts to Love His Neighbours

My neighbours do not wish to be loved.
They have made it clear that they prefer to
        go peacefully
about their business and want me to do the same.
This ought not to surprise me as it does;
I ought to know by now that most people have a
        hundred things
they would rather do than have me love them.

There is television, for instance; the truth
        is that almost everybody,
given the choice between being loved and
        watching TV,
would choose the latter. Love interrupts
        dinner,
interferes with mowing the lawn, washing
        the car,
or walking the dog. Love is a telephone
        ringing or a doorbell
waking you moments after you've finally
        succeeded in getting to sleep.

So we must be careful, those of us who were
        born with
the wrong number of fingers or the gift
of loving; we must do our best to behave
like normal members of society and not make
        nuisances
of ourselves; otherwise it could go hard
        with us.
It is better to bite back your tears,
        swallow your laughter,
and learn to fake the mildly self-deprecating
        titter

favoured by the bourgeoisie
than to be left entirely alone, as you will be,
if your disconformity embarrasses
your neighbours; I wish I didn't keep forgetting
    that.

The Fox

For weeks I've heard him barking in the woods
that half encircle the oatfield, each bark
set in a space of silence, like a word
printed on paper. Dogs are drivellers
or blusterers, no doubt because they speak
mostly to humans. This could be the cry
chosen to signal other warriors.

A fox, I've seen him twice, but only when,
preoccupied with something, I've looked up
for no particular reason and seen
a flash of flame just as it has been snuffed out.

My Father's Body Was Found by Children

My father's body was
found by children.
Boys from the neighbourhood
who thought he was asleep
in his chair until
they came back next day
and saw he hadn't moved.
Children often visited him,
I'm told. He'd wrestle
with them if he was drunk,
converse with them soberly
at other times. His shack
was the sort of dwelling
a twelve-year-old would
build for himself,
in his last years he lived
the way a small boy would
if allowed to live alone.
Huck Finn at seventy.

To think he might have been
a child all his life
if less had been asked
of him and more been given.

To think I'm afraid
of him, even now,
half-expecting to look out
some night and see him
standing there:
I fear that most.

This Is What I Wanted to Sign Off With

You know what I'm
like when I'm sick: I'd sooner
curse than cry. And people don't often
know what they're saying in the end.
Or I could die in my sleep.

So I'll say it now. Here it is.
Don't pay any attention
if I don't get it right
when it's for real. Blame that
on terror and pain
or the stuff they're shooting
into my veins. This is what I wanted to
sign off with. Bend
closer, listen, I love you.

The All Night Diner

The man in the next booth pleads for forgiveness.
Each time our eyes meet I read the same questions:
Who am I? How did I get here? What have I done?
What must I do to make you love me again?

And we're almost strangers. Though I've seen enough
to know he's the kind of drunk who can hold down a job
by working twice as hard as anybody else
days he's sober enough to work:
                                    his face is the same
as those of the winos who spend every day
making chin music on the riverbank
back of the Chinese laundry, but their hands are as soft
as a priest's or a banker's. Not his. After forty years
of punching stone walls to prove he's a man,
of clutching that last shred of dignity
that won't let him spill a drop of his hot pork gravy
(first food in three days) though every blood vessel
burst with the effort of keeping the spoon from shaking.
There can come a time
when holding a spoon like a man will save a man's soul.

Confession

Beloved, it frightens me
how all things circle and meet.

I have singled you out
from all the world.

When you lie naked beneath me
or when only our fingertips
touch on the street,
I love you so gently
I become a saint
and would preach to the birds,
had they no better music.

Yet nothing is simple:
all things circle and meet.

The man who took his pleasure
of the young girl's body
and then strangled her
and threw her in a sewer
like a used condom —

there was a moment
before he gave way
to terror
when he studied her knees
like a famished boy,
an instant when he noted
how the spring wind
played with her hair
like young deer in a wheatfield
(he too was a sentimentalist)

and I, beloved,
lightly kissing your breasts
(do you remember, my little jester,
how you told me once
to be less gentle
with the sacred grotto
between your thighs
because, darling, it won't break)

might love you less
if I did not know
that other so well
had not talked with him
far into the night.

The Fat Man's Poem

A fat man is lying on a bed in a furnished room in Pimlico.
He is writing with a mechanical pencil on a sheet torn from
    a child's exercise book.
His writing board is a magazine — at intervals he doodles
    spectacles and moustaches on Elizabeth Taylor,
    Richard Burton and three anonymous models
clad in made-in-America sweaters of washable orlon.

He props himself up on an elbow and writes:
In those days I was as innocent as one of the legendary child-saints
Then, after a pause: *But aren't innocence and sainthood incompatible?*

He lights a cigarette and, from habit, because he has always
    been poor
counts those left in the package.
He wishes he were a painter or a singer,
how he covets the hands and eyes of Paul Klee,
how jealous he is, sometimes, of applause and of money —
though he is thirty-two years old
he plays records with his eyes shut
and pretends it is he who is singing!

So this is one of those who would change the world!
He is very disgusted with himself today
because he has waited for the voices
and they haven't come
    (*pretentious balderdash* he scribbles on his sheet of paper).

Then, suddenly, he writes:
A fat man is lying on a bed in a furnished room in Pimlico.
Soon his pencil is racing across the paper;

and he forgets about cigarettes, forgets about everything,
until it is finished
and he reads what he has written
and doesn't know whether to be proud or ashamed.